THE
intuition
journal

Nourishing daily rituals
to cultivate clarity, inner
wisdom & inspired action

Jo ChunYan

WATKINS
Sharing Wisdom Since 1893

The Intuition Journal
Jo ChunYan

**Dedicated to my parents, who have always held space
for me to follow my intuition.**

Published in the UK and USA in 2019 by Watkins, an imprint of Watkins Media Limited, Unit 11,
Shepperton House, 83–93 Shepperton Road, London N1 3DF
enquiries@watkinspublishing.com

Commissioning Editor: Kelly Thompson
Editor: Susannah Marriott
Head of Design: Georgina Hewitt
Production: Uzma Taj

A CIP record for this book is available from the British Library
ISBN: 978-1-78678-279-3
1 3 5 7 9 10 8 6 4 2

Typeset in Brandon Grotesque

Printed in Slovenia

Note/Disclaimer: The material contained in this book is set out in good faith for general guidance
and no liability can be accepted for loss or expense occurred in relying on the information given. In
particular this book is not intended to replace expert medical or psychiatric advice. This book is for
information purposes only and is for your own personal use and guidance. It is not intended
to diagnose, treat, or act as a substitute for professional medical advice. The author is not a
medical practitioner nor a counsellor, and professional advice should be sought if desired
before embarking on any health-related programme.

a promise to honour yourself

By using The Intuition Journal,
I, _____ promise to:
your name here

△ be curious about whatever arises as I explore my intuition

△ make time for myself every day to do the inner work to allow for transformation and perspective shifts

△ stay open-minded and open-hearted for all that I will learn and all the wisdom that I will receive

△ always hold space for my highest intentions and my higher self

Sign _____ **Date** __.__.__
                                          dd mm yy

understanding intuition

Intuition is your innate inner knowing. As a trained intuition coach, I like to think of it as the wise, guiding voice within that tells us to chase after our wildest dreams – whether to move halfway around the world, start that creative business you've been drawn toward for so long, or just live each day with more simplicity.

You have probably felt that inner nudge or spark that accompanies a stroke of intuition. It may be experienced as a feeling, an energy or a moment of inspired insight. But at its core, tuning into your intuition is simply the act of listening to your body and the whispers of your heart, which is what this journal is designed to help you do.

The benefits of tuning into your intuitive abilities

Your intuition connects you back to what is often described as your higher self – the part of yourself that innately knows what is best for you in the most holistic sense. When you can move through each day from this space, you will feel a deep sense of alignment, and life will become a reflection of your true essence. When you listen to your intuition, you will be able to hold space for the things that support your inner growth, whether that be sitting under a tree to ground yourself, taking an acting class to build inner confidence, or speaking out about an issue for the greater good. Your intuition becomes your life compass, guiding you toward living your truest intention in every moment.

The ability to listen to your intuition is invaluable for many aspects of life – from relationships, communication and problem-solving, to creativity, leadership and business.

When you learn to act from a place that feels deeply aligned with your core values, you will move through life with clarity, meaning and purpose, enabling you to make a more positive impact on the world around you. Albert Einstein, Steve Jobs, Pablo Picasso, Oprah Winfrey and Nicolas Tesla are among the many inspiring figures who have recognized that it was intuition that guided them to do their life-changing work.

How do you know when your intuition is speaking to you?

People sense and experience their intuition in different ways. For some, it might come through as a gentle guiding voice; for others, an inspiring vision. Use the exercise on the following page to get to know how best to recognize intuitive insights in your own life. Learning to listen to a healthy balance of both your heart (intuition) and your head (rationality and logic) will serve you well.

The purpose of this journal

This journal has been created as a dedicated place for you to tune into, develop and act on your intuition by cultivating space and stillness between your thoughts.

Writing in it daily means making a commitment to knowing yourself better and to allowing your innate wisdom to emerge with more clarity. I hope you enjoy the journey of perspective shifts and inner growth that it takes you on – so that you can love and appreciate your life even more than you do already.

With much love from,
Jo

tapping into your intuition

We are all born with intuition and we all have the ability to refine this skill, just like any other innate talent, throughout our lives.

Most people receive intuition through a primary sense that can be called a "clair" sense. You may only have heard this term in the context of psychics and clairvoyants, but if you have ever noticed the feeling change in a room after an argument or sensed the emotion in the text of a letter, you are using your clair senses. To identify your strongest clair sense(s), tick the boxes that best apply to you below. Keep the results of this assessment in mind as you move through the journal, looking for intuitive insights.

Clairvoyance (sight)

◇ I see symbols, visions or vivid dreams in my mind's eye
◇ I express myself naturally by sketching or drawing
◇ I feel drawn to the visual arts, design or photography
◇ I see auras, energy, ghosts or non-physical entities

Claircognizance (knowing)

◇ I experience persistent thoughts or nudges to act
◇ I believe strongly in what I know as the truth
◇ I feel drawn to philosophy, ethics or scientific research
◇ I receive premonitions or unexplainable knowing

Clairaudience (sound)

◇ I feel inspired and moved by music and languages
◇ I express myself naturally through music or speech
◇ I feel drawn to performing, singing, writing or speaking
◇ I find myself hearing sounds with no physical source

Clairalience (smell)

- ◇ I find that scents evoke memories and experiences
- ◇ I have a heightened sensitivity to smell and fragrance
- ◇ I feel drawn to floristry, wine tasting or perfumery
- ◇ I find myself conjuring or sensing an odour with no physical source

Clairgustance (taste)

- ◇ I find that eating conjures up feelings and memories
- ◇ I have a love of cooking and good food
- ◇ I feel drawn to baking, working with food or food writing
- ◇ I find myself conjuring or sensing a taste with no physical source

Clairtangency (touch)

- ◇ I find that objects evoke strong sensations
- ◇ I love working with my hands (woodwork, pottery)
- ◇ I feel drawn to healing with reiki, kinesiology or massage
- ◇ I receive intuitive insight through physical touch

Clairempathy (emotional sensing)

- ◇ I have an acute sense of emotional perception
- ◇ I attune to the emotion of others' feelings and thoughts
- ◇ I feel drawn to acting, therapy or teaching
- ◇ I sense the truth by feeling the energy of it around me

Clairsentience (visceral emotional feeling)

- ◇ I experience strong visceral and physical reactions
- ◇ I feel the emotions of others in my body
- ◇ I feel drawn to healing, nursing or therapy
- ◇ I sense the truth by feeling the energy of it in my body

your intuition journey

This journal is presented in four sections, or phases. Each phase runs for 13 weeks, covering a different stage of emotional and spiritual growth as you develop your intuition over a year.

These four phases echo the natural growth cycle of a seed evolving into a plant or tree. A tiny seed is planted in fertile ground. As it is nourished by nutrients in the soil, its roots anchor down to create a strong foundation, and it sprouts through the earth. The seedling makes its way upwards, leaves opening to catch the sunlight and buds forming. It extends its branches and eventually evolves into a fully grown plant or tree – abundant in fruit and flourishing flowers.

By using this journal each day, you will nurture your intuition in the same way – so that your inner growth and transformation can bring your dreams, intentions and visions to life.

Moving through the phases

△ **Phase One**
Preparing Sacred Ground
Creating a stable and nourishing foundation for your intuitive intentions and insights.

△ **Phase Two**
Nurturing the Seedling
Moving through moments with curiosity and joy, and removing obstacles that inhibit you from connecting to your intuition.

△ **Phase Three**
Navigating Deep Growth
Working through the ego and fear that holds you back from connecting to your higher self.

△ **Phase Four**
Living in Full Flourish
Committing to strengthening your energy to hold space for even deeper inner work.

Moving through the weeks

For each phase in the journal, you will find an initial intention-setting feature, followed by 13 weeks of "Intuition Focus" and "Daily Intuition Journal" pages.

You will also find quotes and pages of additional insight into the theme of intuition in each phase – as extra food for thought.

For best results, begin with Phase One and move through a full year of growth week by week – Intuition Focus followed by Daily Intuition Journal each time.

The pages are not dated so, if you'd rather spend a little more time peeling back the layers, feel free to move through the weeks at your own pace. And, while the order of the pages has been designed to bring you on a gradual journey of transformation,

if you occasionally need to skip an Intuition Focus for some reason, this shouldn't prevent you from going ahead and filling in the next Daily Intuition Journal.

The most important thing is to develop a regular intuition practice in whatever form suits you best and is most sustainable within the context of your wider life.

Keeping an open mind

Throughout the journal you will find practices from a wide range of traditions, so the more open you can be, the better! If a particular practice piques your curiosity, I encourage you to explore it further.

how to use your intuition journal

*The hope is that using this journal will create
a daily intuition ritual that offers you space to
pause, look within and reflect on yourself and your
inner wisdom – developing in the process more
trust, self-belief, clarity and alignment in your life.*

Beginning with intention

At the start of each 13-week phase, you will be given space
to set an overarching intention for the weeks to follow. The
idea is for you to anchor into the feeling and energy you
would like to bring with you on the journey ahead.

In my experience as an intuition coach, I've seen that setting
a heart-led intention, which allows you to embody a feeling
or state of being, is a highly effective approach.

Once you have identified your underlying intention, it can
be woven through your weekly practices and journalling
however feels most supportive.

There are also Intuition Focus pages in each phase dedicated
to reviewing and, if appropriate, resetting your intention
so that you can continue to weave it through your intuition
journey if desired.

Establishing a focus for your intuition

After the initial intention-setting section at the start of each
phase, you will find what is called an Intuition Focus for the
week ahead. These weekly Intuition Focus pages will lead
you through prompts and exercises to explore a particular
aspect of developing your intuition.

At the end of each Intuition Focus, you will be encouraged to choose a key Intuitive Action to hone in on for the week ahead. This is your chance to identify a specific activity from what you have learned so far to put into practice.

It's important to decide upfront on a regular time each week that feels feasible for you to devote time to engaging with these Intuition Focus pages. For example, you might decide that a Sunday night or first thing on a Monday morning is a good time to set yourself up for the rest of the week.

You will see that the Intuition Focus for some weeks are dedicated to free contemplation, allowing you to step back a little and integrate all the inner work you have done.

Then, at the end of each phase, you will find a week purely for reflection – to celebrate your journey so far.

Completing your "Daily Intuition Journal"

After each Intuition Focus, you will always find the Daily Intuition Journal for the week. It is here that you are given the space to write about your intuitive experiences, insights, feelings and actions on a day-to-day basis, with the choice to put as much emphasis as you want on the insights that have arisen from the preceding Intuition Focus work. You will also find space here to track self-care routines and to acknowledge key moments in the week.

These pages are designed to be the core of your Daily Intuition Ritual and the beating heart of your year of intuitive journalling.

creating your daily intuition ritual

Before you turn the page to start Phase One of your intuition journey, it's useful to remember some of the key aims and benefits of cultivating a Daily Intuition Ritual with the help of this journal. Doing so will encourage and empower you to:

△   Spend time tuning into your heart, breath and body, as well as your mind

△   Turn moments of intuitive insight into inspired intuitive action

△   Recognize, tap into and honour your innate wisdom on a daily basis

△   Practise self-care rituals that support your higher self

△   Cultivate an enhanced sense of space, stillness, self-trust and clarity

In order to gain these benefits, it's important to figure out how it's best for you to integrate your journalling – and any other nourishing rituals that emerge from your self-exploration – into your own life. This will help to make the intuitive work something you do as an act of self-love every day. Follow the steps below to help you with this.

Step One ~ Create space in your life

1. Identify a quiet, uncluttered space in your home that you could use for your intuition practice.

2. Is there a particular time at the start of each week that would work best for you to intuitively explore the weekly Intuition Focus?

3. Is there a particular time each day that would feel best for you to fill in your Daily Intuition Journal? How much time do you feel is realistic for this each day?

Step Two ~ Schedule time in your calendar

Based on the thoughts that emerge from Step One, decide on a place and time(s) that would feel most supportive for you. If the same time every week or day doesn't work for you, simply select the times that suit your schedule and add them to your calendar to make them a priority.

Step Three ~ Commit to your practice

To strengthen your dedication to your intuition journey, commit to honouring your daily ritual by signing below.

I, _____ *create space for my Daily Intuition Ritual for*

your name here

_____ *each day.*

duration

time to begin

When you turn the page, you will begin Phase One. I wish you well as you embark on this unique journey of enquiry into your own innate wisdom. May it bring you much joy to watch the seeds of intuition and intention that you plant grow and flourish as you travel through the year.

Phase One

Preparing Sacred Ground

*Your wildest dreams grow
out of fertile earth*

A new beginning comes from the planting of a single seed in fertile ground. Within this seed lies all the potential for new life and growth.

In order for a seed to sprout into a seedling and then develop into a plant, it must be nourished by good soil. If the ground is not rich in nutrients, the seed will struggle to sprout. If the ground is not firm, it will not provide a strong foundation for the roots to anchor into as the plant grows. This is also true when it comes to developing your intuition.

Over the next 13 weeks we will prepare the ground for you – making it feel stable, nourishing and sacred. In this safe, anchored sanctuary you will be able to connect with your inner knowing and use this to nurture your heart-led intentions and wildest dreams.

In this phase, we will explore:

△ Recognizing intuitive messages

△ Knowing your why

△ Three things you need to develop your intuition

△ Grounding your energy

△ Refining your daily ritual

△ Enhancing your practice space

△ Connecting to your higher self

△ Ways to balance your third-eye chakra

△ Cleansing your space

△ Intentionally calling on your intuition

Along the way you will find space both to set and review your intention for the phase. There is also space to reflect, to allow your insights to settle and to celebrate your journey so far.

setting your intention for phase one

Throughout this journal, an intention is a desired feeling, action or state of being that is aligned with your higher self. By taking the time to set an overarching intention for how you would like to feel before starting this phase, you will set the tone and direction for your intuition journey over the next 13 weeks.

What one thing do you feel most aligned to change in your life over the next 3 months?
Example: I want to write a book.

Based on this, my intention for Phase One of my growth is:
Example: I want to express myself freely and to be in creative flow.

Once you you have clarified this intention on the page opposite, it can be woven through your weekly journalling as much – or as little – as you want. You will also have the chance to check in and review it in Week 3 and again in Week 10.

clarifying your intention for phase one

How will living this intention daily make you feel? What will it change or shift?
Example: It will allow me to honour my truth.

What do you need to let go of or release to live your intention?
Example: I need to release the need for my writing to be perfect.

What one thing could you do as an initial step to begin living your intention?
Example: I will set aside 3 hours each Sunday morning to sit and write.

Spending time getting to know your unique intuitive "voice" will make it easier to attune to it as you move through the journal. So let's start this week by bringing more awareness to the tell-tale signs of when your intuition is speaking to you: the micro-sensations, both physical and emotional, that you experience.

What were your top 3 clair senses from the "Tapping into Your Intuition" exercise in the Introduction, so that you can look out for these moving forward?

1.

2.

3.

What do you feel when you experience these clair senses in your body?
Circle the words that apply below or add your own.

Light	*Heavy*	*Hot*	*Cold*
Expansive	*Contracting*	*Persistent*	*Occasional*
Relaxed	*Tight*	*Changeable*	*Grounded*
Tingly	*Dull*	*Certain*	*Clear*
Open	*Closed*	*Focused*	*Diffused*

add your own	add your own	add your own	add your own

Where in your body do you experience physical sensations of intuition?
Example: My heart feels open.

What emotions do you experience when you sense your intuition?
Example: A sense of grounded excitement.

choice of intuitive action for the week

Choose one means (either physical or emotional) of recognizing your
intuitive "voice" that resonates most from the above and actively
look out for this as you move through the week ahead.

daily intuition journal

Use the space on these pages to keep a note of your daily intuitive experiences – moments of intuitive insight, inspired action, and how these make you feel.

Feel free to relate your observations back to your underlying intention for the phase or your choice of intuitive action for the week.

Monday

Tuesday

Wednesday

Self-care Rituals

m	t	w	th	f	s	su
☐	☐	☐	☐	☐	☐	☐
☐	☐	☐	☐	☐	☐	☐

Thursday

Friday

Saturday

Sunday

Weekly Reflection

I felt most connected to myself this week when _____

I listened most to my intuition this week when _____

Let's start this week by exploring your "why" – why does it feel so important to become more in tune with your intuition? This can help to bring more clarity when "listening" for intuitive guidance and create more space for you to delve into the many layers of who you are – in order to spark positive change.

Anchoring Into Your Why – A Guided Meditation

Step One

Sit quietly in a comfortable position. Close your eyes.
Take full, deep breaths in and long, slow breaths out.

Step Two

Notice the sensations in your body. Acknowledge any emotions that rise to the surface. Take a few minutes to sit with the energy of where you are right now.

Step Three

Ask yourself, "Why do I want to lean into my intuition?" and "Why do I seek a deeper connection to myself?" Follow your observations with curiosity and allow yourself to explore whatever feelings and sensations come through for you.

Step Four

When you get the sense that the meditation is complete, open your eyes, bring yourself gently back into the room, then write down your thoughts on the page opposite.

Why is leaning into your intuition important to you?

Why do you seek a deeper connection to yourself?

What would this deeper connection change in your daily life?

choice of intuitive action for the week

Make a commitment to doing this meditation any time this week you
find yourself feeling disconnected or ungrounded. You might even feel like
doing it every day before writing in your Daily Intuition Journal. It's up to you.

daily intuition journal

Use the space on these pages to keep a note of your daily intuitive experiences – moments of intuitive insight, inspired action, and how these make you feel.

Feel free to relate your observations back to your underlying intention for the phase or your choice of intuitive action for the week.

Monday

Tuesday

Wednesday

Self-care Rituals

	m	t	w	th	f	s	su
_____	○	○	○	○	○	○	○
_____	○	○	○	○	○	○	○

Thursday	Friday
Saturday	Sunday

Weekly Reflection

I felt most connected to myself this week when _____

I listened most to my intuition this week when _____

Let's start this week by checking in with the intention that you set at the start of this first phase of growth. Use this time to explore where your intuition now tells you to channel your energy to further cultivate your intention.

How has the intention that you set at the start of Phase One served you so far?
Example: I have written the first two chapters of my book.

What has changed since you consciously identified and started living your intention?
Example: I am expressing my creativity more freely.

What intuitive insights or actions have been most in alignment with your intention so far?
Example: Committing to doing a little writing each weekend.

Take a moment to reflect on your experiences over the past few weeks. If you feel you have shifted your perspective, you may wish to revise your initial intention. Otherwise, rewrite your original intention to recommit to it.

My intention for Phase One of my growth is now:

choice of intuitive action for the week

Based on your answers above, identify one new intuitive action that you could do this week to further nourish the seed of your intention.

daily intuition journal

Use the space on these pages to keep a note of your daily intuitive experiences – moments of intuitive insight, inspired action, and how these make you feel.

Feel free to relate your observations back to your underlying intention for the phase or your choice of intuitive action for the week.

Monday

Tuesday

Wednesday

Self-care Rituals

	m	t	w	th	f	s	su
	☐	☐	☐	☐	☐	☐	☐
	☐	☐	☐	☐	☐	☐	☐

Thursday

Friday

Saturday

Sunday

Weekly Reflection

I felt most connected to myself this week when _____

I listened most to my intuition this week when _____

week ⟨4⟩ **intuition focus**
Integrating your growth

This week let's take a step back to allow some space for feelings and insights to settle in. Consider the seeds of intuition that you have planted so far and how you have nurtured the soil to support your inner growth.

Then use the space below for free journalling, drawing and dreaming. Be guided by your intuition to express yourself in any way that emerges, whether through words, colours, images or anything else that reflects how you feel.

daily intuition journal

Use the space on these pages to keep a note of your daily intuitive experiences – moments of intuitive insight, inspired action, and how these make you feel.

Feel free to relate your observations back to your underlying intention for the phase or your choice of intuitive action for the week.

Monday

Tuesday

Wednesday

Self-care Rituals

	m	t	w	th	f	s	su
	☐	☐	☐	☐	☐	☐	☐
	☐	☐	☐	☐	☐	☐	☐

Thursday	Friday

Saturday	Sunday

Weekly Reflection

I felt most connected to myself this week when _____

I listened most to my intuition this week when _____

Deep inner
work starts
with the
planting
of a single,
intentional
seed.

Three things you need to develop your intuition

Firm Foundation

The discipline of regular practice creates a grounded, structured, sacred container for your intuition to grow in. When you feel safe, centred and anchored, you have the freedom to rise above distracting mind chatter and gut-instinct survival reactions.

Lack of Obstacles

Recognizing and releasing old beliefs and habits that are not in alignment with your higher purpose helps to remove the emotional obstacles preventing you from being able to tune into your intuition, like a plant being blocked from catching the sunlight that it needs to grow.

Strong Connection to the Self

Doing regular self-enquiry work to cultivate a deeper understanding of yourself and the energy around you helps you to create a strong channel for receiving your intuition more clearly.

week ⟨5⟩ intuition focus
Grounding your energy

Let's start this week by exploring practices that will help you to ground your energy. Feeling grounded is integral to an effective Daily Intuition Ritual as it brings awareness back into your body, helping you to feel more centred and calm.

You may need grounding if you feel:

scattered, frustrated, flighty, unfocused, anxious, reactive, disconnected, listless, rushed, out of your body, overwhelmed with thoughts or ideas, overly focused on external outcomes

What grounding activities do you currently do or would you like to explore that could help you to feel more anchored, centred and grounded?
See the page opposite for suggestions to draw from.

choice of intuitive action for the week

Choose one new grounding practice from above that intuitively resonates with you and commit to integrating it into your daily life for the week ahead.

In Nature

Gardening and tending to vegetables

Forest bathing or simply sitting at the foot of a tree

Walking barefoot or wearing footwear made from natural materials

Visualizing your heartbeat connecting to the pulse of the earth

At Home

Bringing earth elements into your home, such as terracotta and stone

Cooking with root vegetables, such as beet, pumpkin, potato and carrot

Using grounding spices and herbs, such as rosemary, ginger and clove

Sleeping on a futon and sitting on the floor instead of a chair

Body-based Practices

Taking an earthing bath with a generous cup of Epsom salts

Spending time at a hot spring

Massaging your back, legs and feet

Doing yoga poses such as Child's Pose, Triangle Pose and Mountain Pose

Other Grounding Practices

Playing with clay or making pottery

Bringing crystals such as jasper, garnet or bloodstone into your home

Using essential oils such as vetiver, copaiba, sandalwood and cedarwood

Attending a sacred cacao ceremony

daily intuition journal

	Monday
Use the space on these pages to keep a note of your daily intuitive experiences – moments of intuitive insight, inspired action, and how these make you feel.	
Feel free to relate your observations back to your underlying intention for the phase or your choice of intuitive action for the week.	

Tuesday	*Wednesday*

Self-care Rituals

	m	t	w	th	f	s	su
_____	◯	◯	◯	◯	◯	◯	◯
_____	◯	◯	◯	◯	◯	◯	◯

week ⟨5⟩

Thursday	Friday

Saturday	Sunday

Weekly Reflection

I felt most connected to myself this week when ＿＿＿＿＿＿＿＿＿＿＿

I listened most to my intuition this week when ＿＿＿＿＿＿＿＿＿＿＿

Let's start this week by considering how you would like the regular time that you dedicate to your intuition practice to look and feel – and how you could refine your Daily Intuition Ritual to help with this.

What feelings do you want to cultivate more of during your Daily Intuition Ritual? *Circle the words that apply below or add your own.*

Fulfilled	*Content*	*Loving*	*Reflective*
Calm	*Relaxed*	*Inspired*	*Refreshed*
Still	*Connected*	*Healthy*	*Vulnerable*
Clear	*Focused*	*Energised*	*Gentle*

add your own	add your own	add your own	add your own

What 2 or 3 simple things could you do during your Daily Intuition Ritual to help you experience more of these feelings?
Example: Savour a cup of my favourite tea, without distractions.

Which self-care practices help you to feel an enhanced sense of stillness that could allow you to tune in more to your intuition?
Example: Taking a hot bath, journalling, meditating.

How can you honour your Daily Intuition Ritual on days when you feel tired or busy?
Example: Remind myself that this is when I need to do it the most.

choice of intuitive action for the week

Choose one of the ways identified above to enhance your Daily Intuition Ritual and make an active effort to weave it into the week ahead.

daily intuition journal

Use the space on these pages to keep a note of your daily intuitive experiences – moments of intuitive insight, inspired action, and how these make you feel.

Feel free to relate your observations back to your underlying intention for the phase or your choice of intuitive action for the week.

Monday

Tuesday

Wednesday

Self-care Rituals

	m	t	w	th	f	s	su
_____	☐	☐	☐	☐	☐	☐	☐
_____	☐	☐	☐	☐	☐	☐	☐

Thursday

Friday

Saturday

Sunday

Weekly Reflection

I felt most connected to myself this week when _____

I listened most to my intuition this week when _____

Let's start this week by turning your attention to the place in your home where you do your Daily Intuition Ritual. On the page opposite is a list for you to explore of ways in which you could enhance this space to deepen your practice.

A few top sanctuary tips

△   Ensure the space you use for your daily practice is clutter-free.

△   Set your energetic intention to use the space for contemplation, stillness and connection with your inner wisdom and higher self.

△   Wear the same clothes every time you practise your Daily Intuition Ritual to anchor it into a habit.

△   If your home allows for it, you may like to use a space in the northeast corner – the area of spiritual development according to Feng Shui.

choice of intuitive action for the week

Choose three of the suggestions opposite that you feel most drawn to and introduce them into your practice space – your sanctuary – as you move through the week ahead and beyond.

What could you introduce into your sanctuary to cultivate more calm?

◇ Essential oils
◇ Incense
◇ Candles
◇ Lighting
◇ Altar
◇ _____
◇ _____

add your own

details / notes
_____
_____
_____
_____
_____
_____
_____

Which elements from nature could deepen your sense of connection to your intuition?

◇ Plants
◇ Crystals
◇ Water
◇ Wood
◇ Ceramics
◇ _____
◇ _____

add your own

details / notes
_____
_____
_____
_____
_____
_____
_____

What other objects would be supportive for developing your intuition?

◇ Notebook or journal
◇ Tarot or Oracle deck
◇ Nourishing books
◇ Yoga mat
◇ Meditation cushion
◇ _____
◇ _____

add your own

details / notes
_____
_____
_____
_____
_____
_____
_____

daily intuition journal

Use the space on these pages to keep a note of your daily intuitive experiences – moments of intuitive insight, inspired action, and how these make you feel.

Feel free to relate your observations back to your underlying intention for the phase or your choice of intuitive action for the week.

Monday

Tuesday

Wednesday

Self-care Rituals

	m	t	w	th	f	s	su
_____	☐	☐	☐	☐	☐	☐	☐
_____	☐	☐	☐	☐	☐	☐	☐

Thursday	*Friday*
Saturday	*Sunday*

Weekly Reflection

I felt most connected to myself this week when _____

I listened most to my intuition this week when _____

intuition focus
Connecting to your higher self

Practising the Higher Self Embodiment Ritual on the page opposite at the start of this week will help you to tune into the energy of what it feels like to be at your most authentic and intuitive. This embodiment of your higher self, as noted at the top of the pyramid below, will bring you closer to the truest, purest, most complete version of yourself.

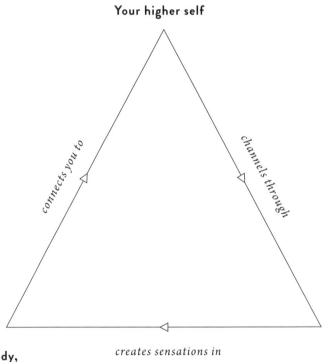

The Intuition Pyramid

Your higher self

connects you to

channels through

creates sensations in

Your body, emotions, energy

Your intuition

Take a few moments to settle into your breath. Tune into a moment when you felt at your most expansive and truthful. This is your higher self.

Describe this moment in detail – the sensations you felt in your body, your emotions, thoughts and actions:

choice of intuitive action for the week

Make a commitment to look out for the above aspects of your higher self as you move through the week ahead and do something every day to cultivate this further.

daily intuition journal

Week Starting ___ . ___ . ___
dd   mm   yy

Use the space on these pages to keep a note of your daily intuitive experiences – moments of intuitive insight, inspired action, and how these make you feel.

Feel free to relate your observations back to your underlying intention for the phase or your choice of intuitive action for the week.

Monday

Tuesday

Wednesday

Self-care Rituals

	m	t	w	th	f	s	su
_____	☐	☐	☐	☐	☐	☐	☐
_____	☐	☐	☐	☐	☐	☐	☐

Thursday

Friday

Saturday

Sunday

Weekly Reflection

I felt most connected to myself this week when _____

I listened most to my intuition this week when _____

How do you
nurture
the soil and
support the
foundation on
which your
dreams grow?

Ways to balance your third-eye chakra

According to ancient Indian tradition, the energy centre between the brows – known as the third-eye chakra (or *ajna* chakra in Sanskrit) – is associated with inner vision and wisdom. Bringing this into energetic balance will cultivate a stronger sense of intuition and connection to self.

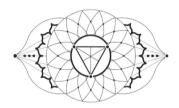

To bring into balance

△ Nourish yourself with purple foods (the colour associated with the third-eye chakra), such as figs, aubergine (eggplant), plums, blueberries, blackberries, purple grapes, plus cacao for mental clarity.

△ Connect with nature by spending time in the sun, moonlight bathing or star gazing.

△ Practise self-awareness by observing your thoughts, tracking any visualizations and keeping a dream journal.

△ Practise meditation and yoga poses such as Child's Pose and Standing Half-forward Bend.

This week it's time to allow some space for your feelings and insights to settle, and for changes to embed. Reflect on how your sensitivity to tuning in and listening to your intuition has evolved.

Then use the space below for free journalling, drawing and dreaming in any way you feel drawn to.

daily intuition journal

Use the space on these pages to keep a note of your daily intuitive experiences – moments of intuitive insight, inspired action, and how these make you feel.

Feel free to relate your observations back to your underlying intention for the phase or your choice of intuitive action for the week.

Monday

Tuesday

Wednesday

Self-care Rituals

	m	t	w	th	f	s	su
	☐	☐	☐	☐	☐	☐	☐
	☐	☐	☐	☐	☐	☐	☐

Thursday

Friday

Saturday

Sunday

Weekly Reflection

I felt most connected to myself this week when _____

I listened most to my intuition this week when _____

intuition focus
Reviewing your Phase One intention

Let's start this week by checking in with the intention that you reviewed in Week 3. Use this time to reflect on any changes you have noticed, no matter how small, and to explore where your intuition now tells you to channel your energy to further cultivate your intention.

How has the intention that you set served you since the review in Week 3?
Example: I finished the first draft of my book.

What has changed for you since the last review?
Example: I have more clarity around my creative style and my voice.

What intuitive insights or actions have been most in alignment with your intention so far?
Example: I am writing the book that I have wanted to write for years.

Take a moment to reflect on your experiences over the past few weeks. If you feel you have shifted your perspective, you may wish to revise your initial intention. Otherwise, rewrite your original intention to recommit to it.

My intention for Phase One of my growth is now:

choice of intuitive action for the week

Based on your answers above, identify one new intuitive action that you could do this week to further nourish the seed of your intention.

daily intuition journal

Use the space on these pages to keep a note of your daily intuitive experiences – moments of intuitive insight, inspired action, and how these make you feel.

Feel free to relate your observations back to your underlying intention for the phase or your choice of intuitive action for the week.

Monday

Tuesday

Wednesday

Self-care Rituals

	m	t	w	th	f	s	su
	○	○	○	○	○	○	○
	○	○	○	○	○	○	○

Thursday

Friday

Saturday

Sunday

Weekly Reflection

I felt most connected to myself this week when _____

I listened most to my intuition this week when _____

intuition focus
Cleansing your space

As you become more intuitively sensitive, it becomes important to cleanse your dedicated practice space of any stagnant or negative energy in order to nourish your intuitive abilities. So let's begin this week by exploring some rituals for cleansing your sanctuary. See the page opposite for suggestions.

When to cleanse your space

△   Before practising your Daily Intuition Ritual

△   When you start or complete a project

△   If you feel tired, stressed, sad or anxious

△   After a guest leaves your home

△   After physically cleaning your space

△   Following sickness, conflict or an accident

△   When the space feels energetically heavy or stagnant

△   At the beginning of a new season

△   At the new moon and full moon

Physical Rituals

Open the windows, declutter and welcome new energy into your home.

Clearing	dust and remove old objects that block energy flow
Crystal	place selenite on a windowsill
Salt	sprinkle salt in corners, or switch on a salt lamp

Aromatic Rituals

Diffuse oils in your space, and smudge incense or herb smoke through your aura.

Essential Oils	lavender, cedarwood, lemon, basil
Herbs	white sage, sustainable palo santo, bay leaves
Incense	sandalwood, frankincense, myrrh, amber

Energetic Rituals

Cleanse and enhance the positive energy of your space with sound vibration.

Singing bowl	play during meditation to clear and align energy
Tingsha bells	let their pure, high tone move stagnant energy
Mantra	repeat your choice of positive powerful words to raise the vibrational energy

choice of intuitive action for the week

Choose two or three of the cleansing rituals above and commit to doing them to boost your ability to tune inward as you move through the week ahead.

daily intuition journal

Week Starting __ . __ . __
dd · mm · yy

Use the space on these pages to
keep a note of your daily intuitive
experiences – moments of intuitive
insight, inspired action, and how
these make you feel.

Feel free to relate your observations
back to your underlying intention
for the phase or your choice of
intuitive action for the week.

Monday

Tuesday

Wednesday

Self-care Rituals

	m	t	w	th	f	s	su
	☐	☐	☐	☐	☐	☐	☐
	☐	☐	☐	☐	☐	☐	☐

Thursday	Friday

Saturday	Sunday

Weekly Reflection

I felt most connected to myself this week when _____

I listened most to my intuition this week when _____

intuition focus
Intentionally calling on your intuition

Let's start this week by exploring how we can purposefully call on our intuition to feel into particular problems or concerns that arise in our lives, rather than only waiting for moments of intuitive insight to come to us.

Step One ~ Identify and understand your concern

Close your eyes, slow your breath and take a moment to still your thoughts. Bring a current question or issue that you would like intuitive guidance on into your awareness. Connect with its energy. Then list the emotions that come up for you:

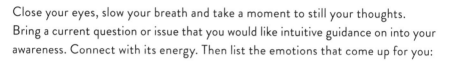

Describe what these emotions mean for you and where you feel they come from:

Step Two ~ Embody the emotions

Visualize how you would feel if you could move through these emotions. Recognize the sensations that appear in your body and describe them:

Step Three ~ Take intuitive action

Ask yourself what intuitive actions you need to take to move through these emotions with integrity and write down your intuitive responses:

choice of intuitive action for the week

Commit to using this three-step process any time you feel you could do with intuitive guidance as you move through the week ahead.

daily intuition journal

Use the space on these pages to keep a note of your daily intuitive experiences – moments of intuitive insight, inspired action, and how these make you feel.

Feel free to relate your observations back to your underlying intention for the phase or your choice of intuitive action for the week.

Monday

Tuesday

Wednesday

Self-care Rituals

	m	t	w	th	f	s	su
	○	○	○	○	○	○	○
	○	○	○	○	○	○	○

Thursday

Friday

Saturday

Sunday

Weekly Reflection

I felt most connected to myself this week when _____

I listened most to my intuition this week when _____

Now that you've reached the end of this first phase of your intuition journey, let's start this week by acknowledging and celebrating all that you have learned and nurtured over the past 12 weeks. Reflect back on how you have cultivated:

Δ   a deeper understanding of your intuition

Δ   a sense of grounding and anchoring into sacred space

Δ   a foundational, intuitive daily ritual practice

Δ   deeper connection to your higher self

Now sit quietly, tune into your breath and respond to these prompts:

What did you learn about how your intuition speaks to you in Phase One?

How did you use your intuition to anchor your intention for Phase One?

3 key times your intuition guided you as you made a decision:

1.

2.

3.

3 key things you manifested by taking intuitive action:

1.

2.

3.

3 key challenges or fears you overcame by following your intuition:

1.

2.
3.

choice of intuitive action for the week

What have you done as a result of following your intuition throughout Phase One that you are most proud of and grateful for? And why do you think that is? Make a choice to honour this by carrying the energy of it into the week ahead and seeing how this makes you feel.

daily intuition journal

Use the space on these pages to keep a note of your daily intuitive experiences – moments of intuitive insight, inspired action, and how these make you feel.

Feel free to relate your observations back to your underlying intention for the phase or your choice of intuitive action for the week.

Monday

Tuesday

Wednesday

Self-care Rituals

	m	t	w	th	f	s	su
_____	◯	◯	◯	◯	◯	◯	◯
_____	◯	◯	◯	◯	◯	◯	◯

Thursday	Friday
Saturday	Sunday

Weekly Reflection

I felt most connected to myself this week when _____

I listened most to my intuition this week when _____

Phase Two

Nurturing the Seedling

*Weave your own path toward
the things that nourish you*

A seed, when nurtured, sprouts through the ground and evolves into a curious seedling, which, in turn, starts to explore its environment, weaving and stretching upwards from the forest floor in search of sunlight.

This is also true of your own growth. May the image of the young curious seedling inspire you to connect back to your inner child and explore the world with more of a sense of wonder.

In the 13 weeks of this second phase of your intuition journey, we will nurture your inner child and help you to intuitively tune into this aspect of yourself using activities that soothe and bring greater connection, creativity and joy. You will also deepen your inner work through supportive rituals that help to release old habits, clearing a path for you to grow and expand.

In this phase, we will explore:

△ Creating an anchoring evening ritual

△ Creating an anchoring morning ritual

△ Questions to help with everyday decisions

△ Connecting to your inner child

△ Soothing your inner child

△ Playing with curiosity

△ Finding joy in simplicity

△ Questions to help with life-changing decisions

△ Identifying old habits

△ Releasing old habits

Along the way you will find space both to set and review your intention for the phase. There is also space to reflect, to allow your insights to settle and to celebrate your journey so far.

setting your intention for phase two

Throughout this journal, an intention is a desired feeling, action or state of being that is aligned with your higher self. By taking the time to set an overarching intention for how you would like to feel before starting this phase, you will set the tone and direction for your intuition journey over the next 13 weeks.

What one thing do you feel most aligned to change in your life over the next 3 months? This can be related to your intention for Phase One or something new. *Example: I want to eat intuitively for my health.*

Based on this, my intention for Phase Two of my growth is:
Example: I want to feel healthy and energetically balanced.

Once you have clarified this intention on the page opposite, it can be woven through your weekly journalling as much – or as little – as you want. You will also have the chance to check in and review it in Week 16 and again in Week 23.

clarifying your intention for phase two

How will living this intention daily make you feel? What will it change or shift?
Example: It will allow me to feel nourished and connected to my body.

What do you need to let go of or release to live your intention?
Example: I need to stop eating to comfort my emotions.

What one thing could you do as an initial step to begin living your intention?
Example: I will eat without distractions at mealtimes.

Let's start this week by finding a ritual that helps you to unwind at the end of a busy day and connect into the natural energy of the evening. You may want to bear in mind that according to India's ancient Ayurvedic system of wellbeing, going to bed before 10pm – when the slow, heavy, quiet qualities of Kapha energy are at their highest – encourages deeper rest.

What could you do to disconnect from the day with grace and reverence?
Example: Switch off all my devices at 9pm.

What do you intuitively feel could enhance your sense of restfulness at night?
Example: Reading something nurturing before bed.

What could change in your life if you made a nightly ritual of the activities above?
Example: I would wake up feeling well rested and clear in my mind.

If you like the idea of creating an "anchoring evening ritual", using the 40-day tracker below could be a good way to make it into a longer-term habit. Feel free to use the rest of the space below for observations along the way.

1	2	3	4	5	6	7	8	9	10
11	12	13	14	15	16	17	18	19	20
21	22	23	24	25	26	27	28	29	30
31	32	33	34	35	36	37	38	39	40

choice of intuitive action for the week

Try at least one of the restful activities that you identified on the page opposite every night this week and see how it helps to ease you into the night.

daily intuition journal

Use the space on these pages to keep a note of your daily intuitive experiences – moments of intuitive insight, inspired action, and how these make you feel.

Feel free to relate your observations back to your underlying intention for the phase or your choice of intuitive action for the week.

Monday

Tuesday

Wednesday

Self-care Rituals	m	t	w	th	f	s	su
_____	☐	☐	☐	☐	☐	☐	☐
_____	☐	☐	☐	☐	☐	☐	☐

week ⟨14⟩

Thursday	Friday

Saturday	Sunday

Weekly Reflection

I felt most connected to myself this week when _____

I listened most to my intuition this week when _____

intuition focus
Creating an anchoring morning ritual

Let's start this week by considering echoing your evening ritual with an anchoring morning ritual. Make space to connect back to your sense of higher self as you wake from sleep by finding alignment with the natural energy of the morning. According to India's ancient Ayurvedic system of wellbeing, rising before the sun and doing a little yoga or breathwork when the dry, cool, airy qualities of Vata energy are highest, eases you into the day with greater clarity and vitality.

What could you do to help yourself begin each day with purpose and intention?
Example: Physical stretching followed by a positive visualization meditation.

What would make you feel refreshed, energized and inspired?
Example: A gentle yoga practice to build energy.

What could change in your life if you made a morning ritual of the activies above?
Example: I would wake up feeling productive and excited to begin the day.

If you like the idea of an "anchoring morning ritual", using the 40-day tracker below could be a good way to make it into a longer-term habit.

Feel free to use the rest of the space below for observations along the way.

1	2	3	4	5	6	7	8	9	10
11	12	13	14	15	16	17	18	19	20
21	22	23	24	25	26	27	28	29	30
31	32	33	34	35	36	37	38	39	40

choice of intuitive action for the week

Commit to trying at least one of the enlivening activities that you identified on the page opposite this week and see how it enhances your day.

daily intuition journal

Use the space on these pages to keep a note of your daily intuitive experiences – moments of intuitive insight, inspired action, and how these make you feel.

Feel free to relate your observations back to your underlying intention for the phase or your choice of intuitive action for the week.

Monday

Tuesday

Wednesday

Self-care Rituals

	m	t	w	th	f	s	su
_____	☐	☐	☐	☐	☐	☐	☐
_____	☐	☐	☐	☐	☐	☐	☐

Thursday	Friday

Saturday	Sunday

Weekly Reflection

I felt most connected to myself this week when _____

I listened most to my intuition this week when _____

intuition focus
Reviewing your Phase Two intention

Let's start this week by checking in with the intention that you set at the start of this second phase of growth. Use this time to explore where your intuition now tells you to channel your energy to further cultivate your intention.

How has the intention that you set at the start of Phase Two served you so far?
Example: I am cooking all my meals using wholefood ingredients.

What has changed since you consciously identified and started living your intention?
Example: My mind feels clearer.

What intuitive insights or actions have been most in alignment with your intention so far?
Example: I am honouring my body by eating slowly and mindfully.

Take a moment to reflect on your experiences over the past few weeks.
If you feel you have shifted your perspective, you may wish to revise your initial intention. Otherwise, rewrite your original intention to recommit to it.

My intention for Phase Two of my growth is now:

choice of intuitive action for the week

Based on your answers above, identify one new intuitive action that you could do this week to further nurture the seedling of your intention.

daily intuition journal

Week Starting ___ . ___ . ___
                      dd   mm   yy

Use the space on these pages to
keep a note of your daily intuitive
experiences – moments of intuitive
insight, inspired action, and how
these make you feel.

Feel free to relate your observations
back to your underlying intention
for the phase or your choice of
intuitive action for the week.

Monday

Tuesday

Wednesday

Self-care Rituals

	m	t	w	th	f	s	su
_____	☐	☐	☐	☐	☐	☐	☐
_____	☐	☐	☐	☐	☐	☐	☐

Thursday

Friday

Saturday

Sunday

Weekly Reflection

I felt most connected to myself this week when _____

I listened most to my intuition this week when _____

This week let's take a step back to allow some space for feelings and insights to settle in. Consider how you have been nurturing the growth of your intuition, including by exploring new morning and evening rituals.

Then use the space below for free journalling, drawing and dreaming. Be guided by your intuition to express yourself in any way that emerges, whether through words, colours, images or anything else that reflects how you feel.

daily intuition journal

Use the space on these pages to keep a note of your daily intuitive experiences – moments of intuitive insight, inspired action, and how these make you feel.

Feel free to relate your observations back to your underlying intention for the phase or your choice of intuitive action for the week.

Monday

Tuesday

Wednesday

Self-care Rituals

	m	t	w	th	f	s	su
_____	○	○	○	○	○	○	○
_____	○	○	○	○	○	○	○

Thursday

Friday

Saturday

Sunday

Weekly Reflection

I felt most connected to myself this week when _____

I listened most to my intuition this week when _____

The infant
plant sprouts
upwards in
search of
sunlight,
reaching for
the sky.

Questions to help with everyday decisions

Every small decision offers you a gentle way to practise leaning into your intuition. In this second phase of growth, I encourage you to start asking yourself questions like the ones below on a daily basis – not only in an effort to tap more into your innate intuitive ability in order to make decisions, but also to help you to expand your comfort zone and engage in life with a sense of curiosity. Doing so will also help finetune your sensitivity to receiving intuitive messages.

△   What ingredients does my body need to feel nourished today?

△   What colours, textures or scents will cultivate how I want to feel?

△   What information do I want to open my mind to?

△   What kind of movement does my body need today?

△   Does my energy need me to slow down or build momentum?

△   What cup, plate or bowl should I use and where should I eat?

△   Which route should I take to my next appointment?

△   Who do I want to connect with this week?

Let's start this week by contemplating how naturally intuitive we all were as children, before our inner wisdom became clouded by the trappings of the world around us. A wonderful way to develop your intuition is to reconnect with your inner child at a time when you felt loved and nurtured, even if this was not a true reflection of your actual childhood. This creates a sacred container in which your wise inner child can emerge and flourish, knowing that they are whole and complete.

Connecting to Your Inner Child – A Guided Meditation

Step One

Sit quietly in a comfortable position. Close your eyes.
Take full, deep breaths in and long, slow breaths out.

Step Two

Visualize yourself as a young child – in a place and time when
you feel happy, joyful, curious, safe and soothed. Use your
imagination to create a world in which you feel completely loved
and nurtured. Spend as much time as you need filling in the
details of this world of your inner child.

Step Three

What feelings come with experiencing the world as this inner child
version of yourself? Focus in on one of the feelings, intensify it
and allow it to move deeper into your body so you can really feel it.

Step Four

When you get the sense that the meditation is complete, open
your eyes, bring yourself gently back into the room, then
write down your thoughts on the page opposite.

How did it feel to reconnect with your inner child? Did you feel loved, whole and complete?

Did any feelings come through that you have not felt for a long time?

How could you encourage your inner child to be more present in your daily life?

choice of intuitive action for the week

Choose one of the answers to the last question above and commit to integrating this into your life every day for the week ahead to see how it makes you feel.

daily intuition journal

Use the space on these pages to keep a note of your daily intuitive experiences – moments of intuitive insight, inspired action, and how these make you feel.

Feel free to relate your observations back to your underlying intention for the phase or your choice of intuitive action for the week.

Monday

Tuesday

Wednesday

Self-care Rituals

	m	t	w	th	f	s	su
_____	☐	☐	☐	☐	☐	☐	☐
_____	☐	☐	☐	☐	☐	☐	☐

Thursday	Friday

Saturday	Sunday

Weekly Reflection

I felt most connected to myself this week when _____

I listened most to my intuition this week when _____

intuition focus
Soothing your inner child

Let's start this week by reflecting on your experience of reconnecting with your inner child in last week's Intuition Focus. Many people find it difficult as this aspect of themselves has become so hidden by the complex layers of "adult life". However, the more you can hold space to soothe your inner child, the more clearly your intuition will speak through you. As such, exploring the questions below can be invaluable.

How would it feel if you could connect with and soothe your anxious inner child? *Feel free to circle any of the words below or write descriptions of your own below.*

Relaxed	*Comforted*	*Luxurious*	*Nurtured*
Nourished	*Safe*	*Free*	*Loved*
Content	*Warm*	*Protected*	*Vulnerable*

add your own	add your own	add your own	add your own

What self-care rituals would soothe and nurture your inner child?
See the page opposite for suggestions to draw from.

Use soothing *materials*	Enjoy the feeling of freshly laundered bed sheets Use a heavier, weighted blanket for sleep Wear breathable fabrics that wrap you in the feeling of a hug
Bring in a *little warmth*	Allow yourself to be comforted by someone you love Bring out the candles or spend an evening by the fireside Enjoy the ritual of bathing, spending time with your curves
Indulge in *culinary comfort*	Add vanilla, cinnamon or honey to your drinks Take time to savour a piece of chocolate slowly Do a gentle kitchari or other cleanse to soothe digestion
Supercharge *your relaxation* *and meditation*	Cover your eyes with a heated eye pillow in bed Surrender in yoga, in relaxation poses like Corpse Pose Allow whatever needs to come up, accepting all your feelings

choice of intuitive action for the week

Choose two to three of the soothing self-care rituals that you have
identified opposite and weave them into the week that lies ahead,
observing how they make you feel.

daily intuition journal

Use the space on these pages to keep a note of your daily intuitive experiences – moments of intuitive insight, inspired action, and how these make you feel.

Feel free to relate your observations back to your underlying intention for the phase or your choice of intuitive action for the week.

Monday

Tuesday

Wednesday

Self-care Rituals

	m	t	w	th	f	s	su
_____	○	○	○	○	○	○	○
_____	○	○	○	○	○	○	○

Thursday

Friday

Saturday

Sunday

Weekly Reflection

I felt most connected to myself this week when _____

I listened most to my intuition this week when _____

This week let's continue to nurture our inner child by inviting it to come out to play. If we can inject more playful creativity into our lives, we will be able to reconnect with how we were before societal conditioning took place and we became self-conscious about expressing our most heartfelt feelings and desires. May the prompts below help you to reignite your childlike curiosity and open the channel for your intuition to come through.

What did you love to do as a child? What were you naturally good at?
Example: I loved helping my grandmother to bake. I was a natural cook.

What were you particularly drawn to or curious about as a child?
Example: I was fascinated by how my toys were made and put together.

Which activities brought out your sense of play, curiosity and creativity?
Example: Playing and exploring in nature, even if it was just in the garden.

Could you weave any of the activities opposite or above in some way into your everyday adult life?

choice of intuitive action for the week

Choose one of the answers to the last question above and commit
to integrating this action into your life every day in the week ahead
to see how it makes you feel.

daily intuition journal

Use the space on these pages to keep a note of your daily intuitive experiences – moments of intuitive insight, inspired action, and how these make you feel.

Feel free to relate your observations back to your underlying intention for the phase or your choice of intuitive action for the week.

Monday

Tuesday

Wednesday

Self-care Rituals

	m	t	w	th	f	s	su
_____	◯	◯	◯	◯	◯	◯	◯
_____	◯	◯	◯	◯	◯	◯	◯

Thursday

Friday

Saturday

Sunday

Weekly Reflection

I felt most connected to myself this week when _____

I listened most to my intuition this week when _____

intuition focus
Finding joy in simplicity

Let's start this week by exploring the many ways you can bring more joy and pleasure into your day through your senses. This will anchor you back into your body and the childlike bliss of being fully in the present, inspiring you to live with greater connection to your intuition.

Ways to Connect With Joy Through Sensory Exploration

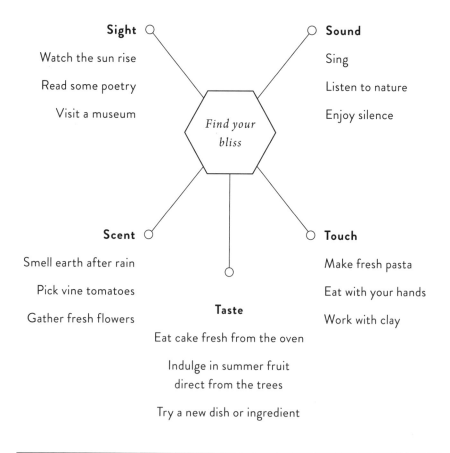

Sight

Watch the sun rise

Read some poetry

Visit a museum

Sound

Sing

Listen to nature

Enjoy silence

Find your bliss

Scent

Smell earth after rain

Pick vine tomatoes

Gather fresh flowers

Touch

Make fresh pasta

Eat with your hands

Work with clay

Taste

Eat cake fresh from the oven

Indulge in summer fruit direct from the trees

Try a new dish or ingredient

What could you do to experience more joy via your senses every day?
See the page opposite for suggestions to draw from but feel free to add your own too.

Sight

Sound

Scent

Taste

Touch

choice of intuitive action for the week

Choose two to three of the activities identified above and weave them into the week that lies ahead, observing how they make you feel.

daily intuition journal

Use the space on these pages to keep a note of your daily intuitive experiences – moments of intuitive insight, inspired action, and how these make you feel.

Feel free to relate your observations back to your underlying intention for the phase or your choice of intuitive action for the week.

Monday

Tuesday

Wednesday

Self-care Rituals

	m	t	w	th	f	s	su
_____	◯	◯	◯	◯	◯	◯	◯
_____	◯	◯	◯	◯	◯	◯	◯

Thursday	Friday

Saturday	Sunday

Weekly Reflection

I felt most connected to myself this week when _____

I listened most to my intuition this week when _____

Every plant
has its own
requirements to
grow but leaves
will always
unfurl to
catch the light.

Questions to help with life-changing decisions

Asking your intuition for guidance when you need to make a big decision will help you to tune into your innermost needs, and provide clarity into how different decisions would serve (or not serve) your higher self. So, when an important decision needs to be made, ask yourself questions like the ones below, allowing your answers to lead you to actions that feel deeply aligned with your truth and values.

△ How do the different options align with my core values?

△ Would any of the options expand my comfort zone?

△ Would any particular decision come from a place of fear?

△ What change do I want to see and embody within myself?

△ How could the different options serve my higher purpose?

3 tips for navigating big decisions

1. Let your intuition set your compass, then allow your head to plan how you get there.

2. Practise patience – it may take time to reach your vision. Trust that everything you encounter on the path will help you to grow.

3. As you move toward your vision, accept each challenge as an opportunity to connect more deeply with your higher self.

intuition focus
Integrating your growth

This week it's time to allow some space for your feelings and insights to settle, and for changes to embed. Reflect on the sensations that arose when you cultivated love, curiosity and joy by connecting to your inner child.

Then use the space below for free journalling, drawing and dreaming in any way you feel drawn to.

daily intuition journal

Use the space on these pages to keep a note of your daily intuitive experiences – moments of intuitive insight, inspired action, and how these make you feel.

Feel free to relate your observations back to your underlying intention for the phase or your choice of intuitive action for the week.

Monday

Tuesday

Wednesday

Self-care Rituals

	m	t	w	th	f	s	su
	○	○	○	○	○	○	○
	○	○	○	○	○	○	○

Thursday

Friday

Saturday

Sunday

Weekly Reflection

I felt most connected to myself this week when _____

I listened most to my intuition this week when _____

Let's start this week by checking in with the intention that you reviewed in Week 16. Use this time to reflect on any changes you have noticed, no matter how small, and to explore where your intuition now tells you to channel your energy to further cultivate your intention.

How has the intention that you set served you since the review in Week 16?
Example: I am now eating more intuitively.

What has changed for you since the last review?
Example: I no longer feel the need to drink alcohol at social gatherings.

What intuitive insights or actions have felt most in alignment with your intention so far?
Example: My energy feels more stable and balanced throughout the day.

Take a moment to reflect on your experiences over the past few weeks. If you feel you have shifted your perspective, you may wish to revise your initial intention. Otherwise, rewrite your original intention to recommit to it.

My intention for Phase Two of my growth is now:

choice of intuitive action for the week

Based on your answers above, identify one new intuitive action that you could do this week to further nurture the seedling of your intention.

daily intuition journal

Use the space on these pages to keep a note of your daily intuitive experiences – moments of intuitive insight, inspired action, and how these make you feel.

Feel free to relate your observations back to your underlying intention for the phase or your choice of intuitive action for the week.

Monday

Tuesday

Wednesday

Self-care Rituals

	m	t	w	th	f	s	su
_____	☐	☐	☐	☐	☐	☐	☐
_____	☐	☐	☐	☐	☐	☐	☐

Thursday	*Friday*

Saturday	*Sunday*

Weekly Reflection

I felt most connected to myself this week when _____

I listened most to my intuition this week when _____

Often when we start to look at our lives a little more closely, we discover that some of our thoughts and actions are actually old habits that no longer serve us. Let's therefore start this week by considering any habits that may be holding you back from a life that feels more aligned to your intuition.

Habits that are no longer serving you may feel:

heavy, stagnant, constraining, energetically draining, like they are keeping you stuck, restrictive, rigid, as if you are moving through the same lessons again and again, in your comfort zone but ready to be released

What habits do you fall into when you are tired, stressed, anxious or uncomfortable? Write down as many of these as come to mind.
Example: I wait until I'm overly hungry and end up snacking as I cook.

Which of these habits do you feel ready to release?

What difference would releasing these habits make to your life?
Example: I'd enjoy cooking and eating my meals more.

choice of intuitive action for the week

Choose one or two of the old habits identified above and, in the week ahead, pay particular attention to when they occur and how it would feel to shift and release these.

daily intuition journal

Use the space on these pages to keep a note of your daily intuitive experiences – moments of intuitive insight, inspired action, and how these make you feel.

Feel free to relate your observations back to your underlying intention for the phase or your choice of intuitive action for the week.

Monday

Tuesday

Wednesday

Self-care Rituals

	m	t	w	th	f	s	su
	○	○	○	○	○	○	○
	○	○	○	○	○	○	○

Thursday	Friday

Saturday	Sunday

Weekly Reflection

I felt most connected to myself this week when _____

I listened most to my intuition this week when _____

intuition focus
Releasing old habits

Following on from last week's focus of identifying old habits that no longer serve you, let's start this week by exploring how you could begin to release these one at a time. This takes a lot of self-awareness and discipline because, once a neural pathway for a repeated behaviour has formed, it tends to happen on autopilot. But the sense of satisfaction you get from ultimately living more in line with your intuition and truest intentions will make it worth the effort.

Step One ~ Identify an old habit

What one habit do you feel ready to release?
Example: Leaving things to the last minute.

Step Two ~ Identify and explore your triggers

What do you feel the main triggers for this habit are?
Example: Believing I can fit more than is possible into any given amount of time.

What first steps could you take to start to overcome these triggers?
Example: Recognize that the belief often ends in stress and worry.

Step Three ~ Take steps toward a new, healthier pattern

What inspired actions could you take to stop the negative habitual behaviour?
Example: Set aside time each night to create a realistic schedule for the next day.

choice of intuitive action for the week

Choose one of the inspired actions that you identified above and commit to doing this every day in the week ahead to see how it starts to change things for you, even if only little by little.

daily intuition journal

Use the space on these pages to keep a note of your daily intuitive experiences – moments of intuitive insight, inspired action, and how these make you feel.

Feel free to relate your observations back to your underlying intention for the phase or your choice of intuitive action for the week.

Monday

Tuesday

Wednesday

Self-care Rituals

	m	t	w	th	f	s	su
	☐	☐	☐	☐	☐	☐	☐
	☐	☐	☐	☐	☐	☐	☐

Thursday

Friday

Saturday

Sunday

Weekly Reflection

I felt most connected to myself this week when _____

I listened most to my intuition this week when _____

intuition focus
Reflecting back on Phase Two

Now that you've reached the end of this second phase of your intuition journey, let's start this week by acknowledging and celebrating all that you have learned and nurtured over the past 12 weeks. Reflect back on how you have explored:

Δ   anchoring morning and evening rituals to enhance each day

Δ   a deeper connection to your wise, playful inner child

Δ   ways to inject more curiosity, simplicity and joy into everyday life

Δ   ways to identify and release old habits that are no longer helpful for you

Now sit quietly, tune into your breath and respond to these prompts:

What did you learn about how your intuition speaks to you in Phase Two?

How did you use your intuition to nurture your intention for Phase Two?

3 key times your intuition guided you as you made a decision:

1.

2.

3.

3 key things you manifested by taking intuitive action:

1.

2.

3.

3 key challenges or fears you overcame by following your intuition:

1.

2.

3.

choice of intuitive action for the week

What have you done as a result of following your intuition throughout
Phase Two that you are most proud of and grateful for? And why
do you think that is? Make a choice to honour this by carrying the
energy of it into the week ahead and seeing how this makes you feel.

daily intuition journal

Use the space on these pages to keep a note of your daily intuitive experiences – moments of intuitive insight, inspired action, and how these make you feel.

Feel free to relate your observations back to your underlying intention for the phase or your choice of intuitive action for the week.

Monday

Tuesday

Wednesday

Self-care Rituals

	m	t	w	th	f	s	su
_____	○	○	○	○	○	○	○
_____	○	○	○	○	○	○	○

Thursday	Friday
Saturday	Sunday

Weekly Reflection

I felt most connected to myself this week when _____

I listened most to my intuition this week when _____

Phase Three

Navigating Deep Growth

*Trust in the unravelling and
extend your branches to the stars*

At a certain stage in a seedling's growth, blossoming slowly commences. This is the result of deep inner transformation – an incubation that is not always visible from the outside.

Just like that seedling, you have the opportunity in this third phase of your intuition journey to undergo deep transformation and blossom. The experience may feel a little challenging and unsettling at times as it nudges you to release long-held beliefs and thought patterns that have been with you most of your life.

During this 13-week phase, you will work on delving into your "shadow side" (the side of ourselves that most people try to hide from the world) so that you can accept all of what makes you the person you are, in turn, helping you tap into the entirety of your intuition.

In this phase, we will explore:

△ Aligning with the seasons

△ Moving with the natural energy of the day

△ Six tell-tale ego signs

△ Identifying long-held beliefs

△ Moving through stuck beliefs

△ Sensing fear in your body

△ Discerning intuition from ego

△ Instinct versus intuition

△ Delving into your shadow side

△ Accepting and integrating your shadow side

Along the way you will find space both to set and review your intention for the phase. There is also space to reflect, to allow your insights to settle and to celebrate your journey so far.

setting your intention for phase three

Throughout this journal, an intention is a desired feeling, action or state of being that is aligned with your higher self. By taking the time to set an overarching intention for how you would like to feel before starting this phase, you will set the tone and direction for your intuition journey over the next 13 weeks.

What one thing do you feel most aligned to change in your life over the next 3 months? This can be related to your intention for Phase Two or something new. *Example: I want to heal the relationship I have with my body.*

Based on this, my intention for Phase Three of my growth is:
Example: I want to accept and love all aspects of myself.

Once you have clarified this intention on the page opposite, it can be woven through your weekly journalling as much – or as little – as you want. You will also have the chance to check in and review it in Week 29 and again in Week 36.

clarifying your intention for phase three

How will living this intention daily make you feel? What will it change or shift?
Example: It will allow me to show up fully as myself.

What do you need to let go of or release to live your intention?
Example: I need to release my fear of being seen.

What one thing could you do as an initial step to begin living your intention?
Example: I will spend time connecting back to my body in meditation.

intuition focus
Aligning with the seasons

In Ayurveda, India's traditional system of wellbeing, each season has its own energetic qualities according to what is known as its *dosha* (see below). Let's start this week by exploring which seasonal energies you currently feel most influenced by and what self-care practices might help to counteract this so that you can feel more attuned to the energy of nature and with your truest inner self. Which of the below seasons and energies do you most identify with at the moment, either physically or mentally and emotionally?

△ **Autumn**   *Dry, cold, light, airy, rough, movable (Dosha: Vata)*
Pacify with warmth, grounding and supportive practices

△ **Winter**   *Cold, windy, heavy, dry, rough, slow (Doshas: Vata & Kapha)*
Pacify with heat, movement, solace, deep rest, comfort

△ **Spring**   *Warm, soft, gentle, slow, heavy, moist (Dosha: Kapha)*
Pacify with cleansing rituals and make space for something new

△ **Summer**   *Active, intense, fiery, hot, oily (Dosha: Pitta)*
Pacify with cooling, relaxing, quiet, slow activities

What simple activities would feel supportive and counter-balance how you currently feel?
See the page opposite for suggestions to draw from.

choice of intuitive action for the week

Choose one of the balancing activities that you identified above and commit to doing this every day during the week ahead to see if it alters how you feel.

Balancing self-care practices for each season

Autumn

Choose sweet or sour flavours, and eat steamed root vegetables

Wear clothing that deflects the wind and cold

Promote calm and clarity through meditation and breathwork

Practise earthing yoga postures such as Child's Pose or Tree Pose

Spring

Cook with bitter, astringent flavours and season with pungent spices

Clean and declutter your home and donate items that you no longer use

Explore something new or begin a creative project

Allow space for less routine and more spontaneity

Winter

Enjoy hearty soups and spicy curries

Drink ginger tea to build heat

Make use of candles and blankets

Prepare for rejuvenating sleep with an anchoring evening ritual

Try more invigorating exercise

Make time for solace and reflection

Summer

Eat lighter portions and fresh salads

Ease digestion with mint, licorice and fennel teas

Swim in a cool lake or river

Enjoy languid afternoons

Relax your abdomen and solar plexus with yoga postures such as Standing Forward Bend

daily intuition journal

Use the space on these pages to keep a note of your daily intuitive experiences – moments of intuitive insight, inspired action, and how these make you feel.

Feel free to relate your observations back to your underlying intention for the phase or your choice of intuitive action for the week.

Monday

Tuesday

Wednesday

Self-care Rituals

	m	t	w	th	f	s	su
_____	○	○	○	○	○	○	○
_____	○	○	○	○	○	○	○

Thursday

Friday

Saturday

Sunday

Weekly Reflection

I felt most connected to myself this week when _____

I listened most to my intuition this week when _____

intuition focus
Moving with the natural energy of the day

There is a natural cycle of energy throughout each day as well as in the turning of the seasons. Let's start this week by finding out what an average day could look like if you lived in accordance with your suggested Ayurvedic daily routine, known as your *dinacharya*, based on the changing energetic qualities throughout the day.

Choose the activities from below that you feel would bring you back to a more natural, balanced and intuitive state of being. Then write these into the wheel opposite to give yourself a visual guide for your ideal day.

Rituals to support your changing energy throughout the day

△ **Kapha energy** *6am to 10am (sunrise)*
Drink water, enjoy a light breakfast, connect with nature, do light work

△ **Pitta energy** *10am to 2pm*
Have lunch (largest meal), do intense mental work, hold meetings, take a walk, allow time for digestion

△ **Vata energy** *2pm to 6pm*
Do gentle exercise, nourishing yin yoga and creative work, plan for next day

△ **Kapha energy** *6pm to 10pm (sunset)*
Have a light dinner, drink a sleep-enhancing tea such as chamomile, indulge in an anchoring evening ritual, take a long bath, relax

△ **Pitta energy** *10pm to 2am*
Enjoy deep sleep, rest and restoration

△ **Vata energy** *2am to 6am*
Sleep, wake before sunrise, spend time in nature, meditate, go to the bathroom, do light yoga and breathwork

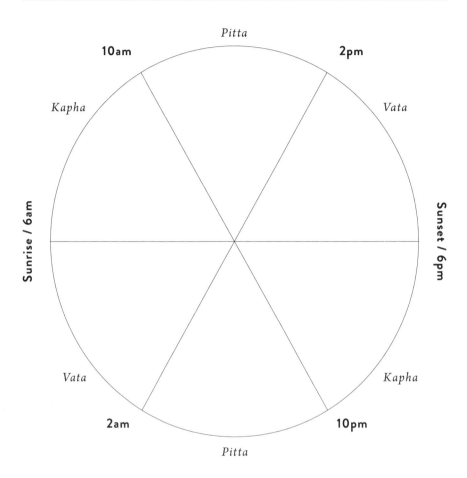

choice of intuitive action for the week

Highlight the activities in the wheel above that could help you to feel more balanced and in tune with your intuition. Then commit to integrating these at the specified times each day during the week ahead.

daily intuition journal

Monday

Use the space on these pages to keep a note of your daily intuitive experiences – moments of intuitive insight, inspired action, and how these make you feel.

Feel free to relate your observations back to your underlying intention for the phase or your choice of intuitive action for the week.

Tuesday

Wednesday

Self-care Rituals

	m	t	w	th	f	s	su
	☐	☐	☐	☐	☐	☐	☐
	☐	☐	☐	☐	☐	☐	☐

Thursday	Friday

Saturday	Sunday

Weekly Reflection

I felt most connected to myself this week when _____

I listened most to my intuition this week when _____

Let's start this week by checking in with the intention that you set at the start of this third phase of growth. Use this time to explore where your intuition now tells you to channel your energy to further cultivate your intention.

How has the intention that you set at the start of Phase Three served you so far?
Example: I feel more confident in my body and take pride in how I dress.

What has changed since you consciously identified and started living your intention?
Example: I am more comfortable standing up and speaking in front of others.

What intuitive insights or actions have felt most in alignment with your intention so far?

Example: I am honouring my shape and curves when I look in the mirror.

Take a moment to reflect on your experiences over the past few weeks. If you feel you have shifted your perspective, you may wish to revise your initial intention. Otherwise, rewrite your original intention to recommit to it.

My intention for Phase Three of my growth is now:

choice of intuitive action for the week

Based on your answers above, identify one new intuitive action that you could do this week to further cultivate your intention.

daily intuition journal

Use the space on these pages to keep a note of your daily intuitive experiences – moments of intuitive insight, inspired action, and how these make you feel.

Feel free to relate your observations back to your underlying intention for the phase or your choice of intuitive action for the week.

Monday

Tuesday

Wednesday

Self-care Rituals

	m	t	w	th	f	s	su
_____	☐	☐	☐	☐	☐	☐	☐
_____	☐	☐	☐	☐	☐	☐	☐

Thursday

Friday

Saturday

Sunday

Weekly Reflection

I felt most connected to myself this week when _____

I listened most to my intuition this week when _____

intuition focus
Integrating your growth

This week let's take a step back to allow some space for feelings and insights to settle in. Consider how you have been nurturing your intuition by becoming more attuned to the natural energy of the seasons and the days according to Ayurvedic energy principles.

Then use the space below for free journalling, drawing and dreaming. Be guided by your intuition to express yourself in any way that emerges, whether through words, colours, images or anything else that reflects how you feel.

daily intuition journal

Use the space on these pages to keep a note of your daily intuitive experiences – moments of intuitive insight, inspired action, and how these make you feel.

Feel free to relate your observations back to your underlying intention for the phase or your choice of intuitive action for the week.

Monday

Tuesday

Wednesday

Self-care Rituals

	m	t	w	th	f	s	su
_____	◯	◯	◯	◯	◯	◯	◯
_____	◯	◯	◯	◯	◯	◯	◯

Thursday

Friday

Saturday

Sunday

Weekly Reflection

I felt most connected to myself this week when _____

I listened most to my intuition this week when _____

Leaves will
fall and
flowers will
wither to
make space
for new
blooms.

Six tell-tale ego signs

When you pursue a vision or a long-held dream, the ego can show up in the form of fear or limiting beliefs – preventing you from hearing and following your intuition.

Asking yourself questions like the ones below can be a useful way to check in with yourself when making decisions. These prompts will help you discern if the predominant voice in your head right now is your ego, scared to venture into the unknown, and therefore trying to keep you in your comfort zone.

1. Am I drawn toward a decision that will fill a superficial need, such as money, status or how people see me?

2. Do I feel that I am grasping for an outcome, rather than allowing myself to naturally move toward it?

3. Do I sense an underlying belief that I am not good or strong enough to pursue your vision?

4. Does the sensation feel draining, heavy and constrictive in my body?

5. Would not pursuing my vision keep me in my comfort zone?

If you answer yes to any of these, it is likely that your ego is indeed at work – encouraging you to act from a place of fear and limitation rather than intuition and joy. If this is the case, choose a path that feels more spacious; one that will take you beyond your comfort zone.

What we learn to believe about ourselves as we grow up has a big influence on how we move through life. Let's start this week by exploring what long-held beliefs and thought patterns (sometimes unconscious) you feel steer you away from acting in alignment with your intuition and your higher self. Next week we will then explore how to move through these stuck beliefs.

Beliefs that are no longer serving you may feel:

controlling, constricting, judgemental, uncompromising, limiting, stuck, like reliving past lessons, from a place where you feel like you aren't enough, ready to be released

Do you have repeated thoughts that do not feel aligned with your highest self?
Example: My body is not beautiful enough.

Do you act out underlying beliefs that no longer seem to serve you?
Example: The belief that I need my attractiveness to be validated by others.

Are there any of these beliefs that you are ready to release?

What difference would releasing this limiting belief make to your life?
Example: A lot of anxious energy would be freed up for creative purposes.

choice of intuitive action for the week

Choose one or two of the beliefs identified above and pay particular
attention to when this occurs during the week ahead and how it
would feel to shift and release it.

daily intuition journal

Use the space on these pages to
keep a note of your daily intuitive
experiences – moments of intuitive
insight, inspired action, and how
these make you feel.

Feel free to relate your observations
back to your underlying intention
for the phase or your choice of
intuitive action for the week.

Monday

Tuesday

Wednesday

Self-care Rituals

	m	t	w	th	f	s	su
	○	○	○	○	○	○	○
	○	○	○	○	○	○	○

Thursday

Friday

Saturday

Sunday

Weekly Reflection

I felt most connected to myself this week when _____

I listened most to my intuition this week when _____

Following on from last week's focus of identifying old limiting beliefs, let's start this week by exploring how you could begin to let go of these one at a time. This may not be a quick or easy process, so take as long as you need. Sometimes, an old belief may evolve and show up as another limiting belief to work through. Keep unravelling this until you reach your core belief. In the end, you will feel free, expansive and able to hear your intuition more clearly.

Step One ~ Identify an old belief that you feel ready to release

The belief you feel ready to release is:
Example: I need to be perfect in order to be loved.

Step Two ~ Identify and explore your triggers

What do you feel the main triggers for this belief are?
Example: When I find flaws in my body and compare it to others'.

Step Three ~ Unravel the belief to its origin

What purpose did this belief originally serve? Acknowledge its reason for being.
Example: I wanted to feel accepted and seen by others.

Step Four ~ Change the experience through inspired action

In the left column, write what you normally do when this belief is triggered.
In the right column, list an alternative action that feels loving and intuitive.

What I currently do

Example: I brush off compliments.

What I could do instead

Example: Say thank you.

choice of intuitive action for the week

Choose one or more of the "inspired actions" that you identified above.
Commit to doing this every day in the week ahead to see how it starts
to change things for you, even if only little by little.

daily intuition journal

Use the space on these pages to keep a note of your daily intuitive experiences – moments of intuitive insight, inspired action, and how these make you feel.

Feel free to relate your observations back to your underlying intention for the phase or your choice of intuitive action for the week.

Monday

Tuesday

Wednesday

Self-care Rituals

	m	t	w	th	f	s	su
	☐	☐	☐	☐	☐	☐	☐
	☐	☐	☐	☐	☐	☐	☐

Thursday	Friday

Saturday	Sunday

Weekly Reflection

I felt most connected to myself this week when _____

I listened most to my intuition this week when _____

intuition focus
Sensing fear in your body

By observing when and how fear shows up in your body, you can begin to recognize when your ego takes hold over your wise, inner self. So let's start this week by doing a meditation to explore the sensation of fear. Be gentle with yourself during the meditation and try to release judgement. If it feels overwhelming, take a step back by returning to the grounding rituals in Phase One or soothing rituals in Phase Two.

Observing Fear – A Guided Meditation

Step One

Sit quietly in a comfortable position. Close your eyes. Take three full, deep breaths in and three long, slow breaths out. Connect into your body with each breath you take.

Step Two

Observe any sensations that arise. Move your attention to your body. Where do you physically feel fear, limiting beliefs and worry? Sit with the energy around these feelings. Focus in on it. Acknowledge and accept any emotions that surface and allow time for them to be processed and released.

Step Three

When you get the sense that the meditation is complete, open your eyes, bring yourself gently back into the room, then write down your thoughts on the page opposite.

How did fear manifest and feel in your body?
Example: I felt a tightness in my throat.

Did any emotions arise that felt like they needed to be processed and released?
Example: I felt lonely, isolated and unheard.

How do you feel now that you have allowed time and space for these emotions to be healed and processed?
Example: I feel lighter and relaxed.

choice of intuitive action for the week

Observe any fear-based sensations that arise in your body as you move through the week ahead and commit to carving out the time to do this meditation to help process and move through these.

daily intuition journal

Week Starting ___ . ___ . ___
dd   mm   yy

Use the space on these pages to keep a note of your daily intuitive experiences – moments of intuitive insight, inspired action, and how these make you feel.

Feel free to relate your observations back to your underlying intention for the phase or your choice of intuitive action for the week.

Monday

Tuesday

Wednesday

Self-care Rituals

	m	t	w	th	f	s	su
_____	○	○	○	○	○	○	○
_____	○	○	○	○	○	○	○

Thursday

Friday

Saturday

Sunday

Weekly Reflection

I felt most connected to myself this week when _____

I listened most to my intuition this week when _____

Although your intuition and your ego (often manifested as fear) speak from very different places, it can, at times, be difficult to discern between the two. Let's start this week by observing the dance between the two and the role that each one plays in this – so that you can learn to acknowledge the presence of your ego without allowing it to direct your decision-making and actions. You will then be able to receive your intuitive nudges with greater clarity.

Think of a situation that you feel you need guidance on and describe it.

My situation is:

Look at this situation from the viewpoint of your ego. What do you fear about the decisions that have to be made?

What self-protective beliefs might be connected to these fears?

Now take a moment to tune into your intuition. What does it guide you to do instead?

choice of intuitive action for the week

When you sense your ego come through during the week ahead, spend a little time sitting with your thoughts. Can you move past it and tune into your intuition instead?

daily intuition journal

Use the space on these pages to
keep a note of your daily intuitive
experiences – moments of intuitive
insight, inspired action, and how
these make you feel.

Feel free to relate your observations
back to your underlying intention
for the phase or your choice of
intuitive action for the week.

Monday

Tuesday

Wednesday

Self-care Rituals

	m	t	w	th	f	s	su
_____	☐	☐	☐	☐	☐	☐	☐
_____	☐	☐	☐	☐	☐	☐	☐

Thursday	Friday

Saturday	Sunday

Weekly Reflection

I felt most connected to myself this week when _____

I listened most to my intuition this week when _____

Beneath a tree, a network of roots extends deep underground. Inner work is not always obvious.

Instinct versus intuition

The words "instinct" and "intuition" are often used interchangeably.
So what is the difference between them?

A moment of instinct is likely to feel like a physiological reaction
that has to be actioned quickly to keep us safe. As with ego, instinct
can often lead us to avoid experiences that feel uncomfortable.
Intuition, on the other hand, tends to channel through with less
urgency, feeling more fluid and open for exploration.

Below is a reminder of the main qualities of each trait. Look
at them now and again to strengthen your ability to tell the
difference between the two.

4 Qualities of Instinct

Δ   Ensures that your basic needs and comforts are met

Δ   Encourages you to choose the safest option

Δ   Has a sense of urgency

Δ   Focuses on the outcome

4 Qualities of Intuition

Δ   Nudges you to expand beyond your comfort zone in order to grow

Δ   Asks you to explore what feels most in alignment to you

Δ   Allows things to unravel fluidly, in their own time

Δ   Focuses on the experience

intuition focus
Integrating your growth

This week it's time to allow some space for your feelings and insights to settle, and for further clarity to channel through. Reflect on how you have been able to identify and move through limiting beliefs and ego-based fears over the past weeks, allowing more inner space to tune into your intuition.

Then use the space below for free journalling, drawing and dreaming in any way you feel drawn to.

daily intuition journal

Use the space on these pages to keep a note of your daily intuitive experiences – moments of intuitive insight, inspired action, and how these make you feel.

Feel free to relate your observations back to your underlying intention for the phase or your choice of intuitive action for the week.

Monday

Tuesday

Wednesday

Self-care Rituals

	m	t	w	th	f	s	su
_____	◯	◯	◯	◯	◯	◯	◯
_____	◯	◯	◯	◯	◯	◯	◯

Thursday

Friday

Saturday

Sunday

Weekly Reflection

I felt most connected to myself this week when _____

I listened most to my intuition this week when _____

intuition focus
Reviewing your Phase Three intention

Let's start this week by checking in with the intention that you reviewed in Week 29. Use this time to reflect on any changes you have noticed, no matter how small, and to explore where your intuition now tells you to channel your energy to further cultivate your intention.

How has the intention that you set served you since the review in Week 29?
Example: I am saying thank you to compliments instead of brushing them off.

What has changed for you since the last review?
Example: I feel more deeply connected to my truth and innermost essence.

What intuitive insights or actions have felt most in alignment with your intention so far?

Example: My posture has changed – I now stand tall with my shoulders back.

Take a moment to reflect on your experiences over the past few weeks. If you feel you have shifted your perspective, you may wish to revise your initial intention. Otherwise, rewrite your original intention to recommit to it.

My intention for Phase Three of my growth is now:

choice of intuitive action for the week

Based on your answers above, identify one new intuitive action that you could do this week to further cultivate your intention.

daily intuition journal

Use the space on these pages to keep a note of your daily intuitive experiences – moments of intuitive insight, inspired action, and how these make you feel.

Feel free to relate your observations back to your underlying intention for the phase or your choice of intuitive action for the week.

Monday

Tuesday

Wednesday

Self-care Rituals

	m	t	w	th	f	s	su
_____	○	○	○	○	○	○	○
_____	○	○	○	○	○	○	○

Thursday	Friday

Saturday	Sunday

Weekly Reflection

I felt most connected to myself this week when _____

I listened most to my intuition this week when _____

Our shadow self is the side of ourselves that we tend to try to hide from the world, scared of how others will judge our "less than" qualities. But by accepting and working with your shadow side, you will become a more authentic version of yourself, and more open to your innate intuition. Let's start this week by exploring your "light" and "shadow" self. Doing this allows for deep healing, so move slowly and if it gets too intense, try the soothing self-care rituals in Phase Two.

Identifying your light and shadow aspects

Light Aspects

Write down the qualities in yourself that you identify as "good" and lovable. *Perbaps these characteristics have defined you or are how you see yourself. Example: Patience, kindness, generosity.*

1.

2.

3.

Shadow Aspects

Write down the qualities in yourself that you identify as "bad" and shameworthy. *These may be characteristics you dislike in others or opposites of your light aspects. Example: Selfishness, laziness, judgemental attitude.*

1.

2.

3.

How do you feel when you see these shadow qualities at play in yourself or others?

When do you notice your shadow side emerge in day-to-day life?

choice of intuitive action for the week

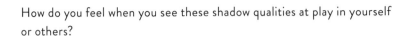

Make a commitment to observing when your shadow side shows up during the week ahead. Be compassionate with yourself and see how this feels.

daily intuition journal

Week Starting ___ . ___ . ___
dd   mm   yy

Use the space on these pages to keep a note of your daily intuitive experiences – moments of intuitive insight, inspired action, and how these make you feel.

Feel free to relate your observations back to your underlying intention for the phase or your choice of intuitive action for the week.

Monday

Tuesday

Wednesday

Self-care Rituals

	m	t	w	th	f	s	su
	☐	☐	☐	☐	☐	☐	☐
	☐	☐	☐	☐	☐	☐	☐

Thursday

Friday

Saturday

Sunday

Weekly Reflection

I felt most connected to myself this week when _____

I listened most to my intuition this week when _____

intuition focus
Accepting and integrating your shadow side

Both your light side and your shadow side are required to make you complete. Neither are inherently good or bad. Each have duality. So let's start this week by looking for the light in your shadow and the shadow in your light. The exercise below will help you to release judgement toward yourself as well as others, freeing you to live more in alignment with your highest self and your truest intentions.

Exploring light and shadow aspects

Think of someone who triggers you in a "negative" way (via their shadow aspects) and someone you admire (via their light aspects), list their characteristics, then respond to the prompts opposite.

Shadow Aspects "negative trigger"

Example: jealous, controlling, lazy

Light Aspects "positive trigger"

Example: kind, warm, forgiving

Which of these light and shadow aspects are ones that you see in yourself?

How have your light aspects inhibited you (creating shadow within the light)?
Example: My kindness stops me from saying no and setting boundaries.

How have your shadow aspects served you (providing light within the shadow)?
Example: Being lazy at times helps me to preserve energy.

choice of intuitive action for the week

Make a commitment to look for the duality in both the light and shadow aspects of yourself and others during the week ahead. See how viewing this with a new sense of balance and compassion makes you feel.

daily intuition journal

Use the space on these pages to keep a note of your daily intuitive experiences – moments of intuitive insight, inspired action, and how these make you feel. Feel free to relate your observations back to your underlying intention for the phase or your choice of intuitive action for the week.	*Monday*
Tuesday	*Wednesday*

Self-care Rituals

	m	t	w	th	f	s	su
_____	☐	☐	☐	☐	☐	☐	☐
_____	☐	☐	☐	☐	☐	☐	☐

Thursday

Friday

Saturday

Sunday

Weekly Reflection

I felt most connected to myself this week when _____

I listened most to my intuition this week when _____

intuition focus
Reflecting back on Phase Three

Now that you've reached the end of the third phase of your intuition journey, let's start this week by acknowledging and celebrating all that you have learned and nurtured over the past 12 weeks. Reflect back on how you have cultivated:

△   energetic balance, by aligning with both the seasonal and daily cycles

△   a better understanding of how ego and fear can hold you back

△   an ability to identify and move through fear and other limiting beliefs

△   compassion for your shadow side and a deeper acceptance of your whole self

Now sit quietly, tune into your breath and respond to these prompts.

What did you learn about how your intuition speaks to you in Phase Three?

How did you use your intuition to nourish your intention for Phase Three?

3 key times your intuition guided you as you made a decision:

1.

2.

3.

3 key things you manifested by taking intuitive action:

1.

2.

3.

3 key challenges or fears you overcame by following your intuition:

1.

2.

3.

choice of intuitive action for the week

What have you done as a result of following your intuition throughout
Phase Three that you are most proud of and grateful for? And why
do you think that is? Make a choice to honour this by carrying the
energy of it into the week ahead and seeing how this makes you feel.

daily intuition journal

Use the space on these pages to keep a note of your daily intuitive experiences – moments of intuitive insight, inspired action, and how these make you feel.

Feel free to relate your observations back to your underlying intention for the phase or your choice of intuitive action for the week.

Monday

Tuesday

Wednesday

Self-care Rituals

	m	t	w	th	f	s	su
_____	◯	◯	◯	◯	◯	◯	◯
_____	◯	◯	◯	◯	◯	◯	◯

Thursday

Friday

Saturday

Sunday

Weekly Reflection

I felt most connected to myself this week when _____

I listened most to my intuition this week when _____

Phase Four

Living
in Full
Flourish

May you flow through each day
wild and in full bloom

Finally, the tree flourishes and blossoms – a beacon of strength, grace and beauty. You, too, will blossom as you start to reap the rewards of the inner work you have done so far.

This final phase of growth is dedicated to guiding you into a state of flourish, from where you can move through life deeply connected to your truth, higher self and deeper purpose. Things may manifest during this phase with more ease and flow now that momentum has gathered.

At the end of these final 13 weeks of your intuition journey, you will know how to access the infinite wisdom of your intuition through your connection to universal energy. The end of this phase will mark the completion of one full cycle of growth. From here, if you continue your inner work with another journal, the cycle of growth will begin again.

In this phase, we will explore:

△   Expanding your comfort zone

△   Inviting in daily discomfort

△   Ways to balance your crown chakra

△   Strengthening your energy body

△   Flowing between yin and yang

△   Balancing your yin–yang energy

△   Flourishing in all areas of life

△   Higher self versus infinite wisdom

△   Channelling infinite wisdom

△   Living in energetic flow

Along the way you will find space both to set and review your intention for the phase. There is also space to reflect, to allow your insights to settle and to celebrate the cylce of growth that you undergo.

setting an intention for phase four

Throughout this journal, an intention is a desired feeling, action or state of being that is aligned with your higher self. By taking the time to set an overarching intention for how you would like to feel before starting this phase, you will set the tone and direction for your intuition journey over the next 13 weeks.

What one thing do you feel most aligned to change in your life over the next 3 months? This can be related to your intention for Phase Three or something new. *Example: I would like to feel more at peace in my everyday life.*

Based on this, my intention for Phase Four of my growth is:
Example: I would like to enhance my connection to my higher purpose in life.

Once you have clarified this intention on the page opposite, it can be woven through your weekly journalling as much – or as little – as you want. You will also have the chance to check in and review it in Week 42 and again in Week 49.

clarifying your intention for phase four

How will living this intention daily make you feel? What will it change or shift?
Example: It will allow me to be of more service to others.

What do you need to let go of or release to live your intention?
Example: I need to let go of any pushing and let things evolve in their own time.

What one thing could you do as an initial step to begin living your intention?
Example: I will meditate daily to embody the energy of my higher self.

Let's start this week by exploring where the boundaries of your comfort zone are and how it would feel to expand these. When working with your intuition, the more you can encourage yourself to step outside the familiar and hold space for things that feel uncomfortable, the more you will invite in new opportunities for inner growth.

Describe a time when you resisted doing something because it felt too challenging or uncomfortable. How did this make you feel?
Example: I was too nervous to speak up at work. This made me feel frustrated and stuck.

Describe a time when you explored beyond your comfort zone and grew. How did it feel to move through the discomfort?
Example: I took acting classes to help build my confidence speaking in front of others.

How could taking action to move beyond your comfort zone serve your
higher self?
Example: It would allow me to feel more expansive and confident in my decisions.

choice of intuitive action for the week

Observe the edges of your comfort zone this week, noting the experiences
that you tend to shy away from because they feel uncomfortable –
and sensing whether you intuitively feel they would help you to grow.

daily intuition journal

Use the space on these pages to keep a note of your daily intuitive experiences – moments of intuitive insight, inspired action, and how these make you feel.

Feel free to relate your observations back to your underlying intention for the phase or your choice of intuitive action for the week.

Monday

Tuesday

Wednesday

Self-care Rituals

	m	t	w	th	f	s	su
_____	◯	◯	◯	◯	◯	◯	◯
_____	◯	◯	◯	◯	◯	◯	◯

Thursday	*Friday*

Saturday	*Sunday*

Weekly Reflection

I felt most connected to myself this week when _____

I listened most to my intuition this week when _____

Let's start this week by exploring small acts that you could introduce into your daily life to expand your comfort zone. Doing something small every day that makes you feel a little uncomfortable can lead to massive shifts in being able to surrender any resistance and tune into your intuition more over time.

Reflecting on the week that has just passed, or further back if needed, think of a moment when you tried to control an outcome in order to feel comfortable. *Example: I can become distant in a relationship because I am scared to be vulnerable.*

What are some small actions that you could take to lean more into discomfort and therefore allow more space for inner growth?
See the page opposite for some starter suggestions to draw from.

In life Declutter and let go of things you've been holding onto.
Go to a new café or somewhere else you don't normally go.
Sign up for a new class that makes you a little nervous.
Make quick intuitive decisions without overanalyzing.
Spend a little longer in meditation than you usually do.

In work Speak up and hold your own space in meetings.
Ask for feedback on your work.
Put yourself forward to do something that will stretch you.
Express what you want, without worrying about the outcome.
Take time to build a skill that you aren't confident in.

In relationships Spend time together allowing for silent pauses.
Speak up when something doesn't feel right.
Explore something new together.
Get out and meet people with different perspectives to yours.
See the beauty in people with different traits to yours.

choice of intuitive action for the week

Choose at least one of the intuitive actions identified on the page
opposite and commit to integrating this into the week ahead. See
how it makes you feel and what emerges from this.

daily intuition journal

Monday

Use the space on these pages to keep a note of your daily intuitive experiences – moments of intuitive insight, inspired action, and how these make you feel.

Feel free to relate your observations back to your underlying intention for the phase or your choice of intuitive action for the week.

Tuesday

Wednesday

Self-care Rituals

         m   t   w   th   f   s   su

_____ ☐ ☐ ☐ ☐ ☐ ☐ ☐

_____ ☐ ☐ ☐ ☐ ☐ ☐ ☐

Thursday

Friday

Saturday

Sunday

Weekly Reflection

I felt most connected to myself this week when _____

I listened most to my intuition this week when _____

Let's start this week by checking in with the intention that you set at the start of this final phase of growth. Use this time to explore where your intuition now tells you to channel your energy to further cultivate your intention.

How has the intention that you set at the start of Phase Four served you so far?
Example: I know to tune into my intuition when things feel out of balance.

What has changed since you consciously identified and started living your intention?
Example: I am moving through my day feeling more connected and aligned.

What intuitive insights or actions have felt most in alignment with your intention so far?
Example: I spend five minutes each morning doing a simple breath meditation.

Take a moment to reflect on your experiences over the past few weeks.
If you feel you have shifted your perspective, you may wish to revise your initial intention. Otherwise, rewrite your original intention to recommit to it.

My intention for Phase Four of my growth is now:

choice of intuitive action for the week

Based on your answers above, identify one new intuitive action that you could do this week to further help you and your intention to flourish.

daily intuition journal

Use the space on these pages to keep a note of your daily intuitive experiences – moments of intuitive insight, inspired action, and how these make you feel.

Feel free to relate your observations back to your underlying intention for the phase or your choice of intuitive action for the week.

Monday

Tuesday

Wednesday

Self-care Rituals

	m	t	w	th	f	s	su
_____	◯	◯	◯	◯	◯	◯	◯
_____	◯	◯	◯	◯	◯	◯	◯

Thursday

Friday

Saturday

Sunday

Weekly Reflection

I felt most connected to myself this week when _____

I listened most to my intuition this week when _____

intuition focus
Integrating your growth

This week, let's take a step back to allow some space for feelings and insights to settle in. Contemplate what you have done so far during this phase to step outside of your comfort zone, giving yourself the chance to grow and flourish.

Then use the space below for free journalling, drawing and dreaming. Be guided by your intuition to express yourself in any way that emerges, whether through words, colours, images or anything else that reflects how you feel.

daily intuition journal

Use the space on these pages to keep a note of your daily intuitive experiences – moments of intuitive insight, inspired action, and how these make you feel.

Feel free to relate your observations back to your underlying intention for the phase or your choice of intuitive action for the week.

Monday

Tuesday

Wednesday

Self-care Rituals

	m	t	w	th	f	s	su
_____	☐	☐	☐	☐	☐	☐	☐
_____	☐	☐	☐	☐	☐	☐	☐

Thursday

Friday

Saturday

Sunday

Weekly Reflection

I felt most connected to myself this week when _____

I listened most to my intuition this week when _____

At last, after
seasons of
growth,
the tree is
abundant
with
flowers.

Ways to balance your crown chakra

According to ancient Indian tradition, the energy centre at the crown of your head – known as the crown chakra (or *sahasrara* chakra in Sanskrit) – is associated with higher wisdom and enlightenment. Bringing this into balance will connect you to the infinite wisdom of the universe, enlivening and inspiring you.

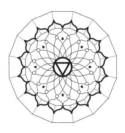

To bring into balance

△ Nourish yourself with a clean and nutritionally balanced, alkalizing diet, rich in fruit and vegetables, and water for purification

△ Connect with nature by spending time in sunlight, and watch the sunrise and sunset when you can

△ Practise being as open and trusting as possible, release the ego and look to infinite wisdom for guidance

△ Practise regular meditation with a focus on the crown chakra, and channel your intuition and wisdom through writing

intuition focus
Strengthening your energy body

We often focus so much on our physical body that it can be easy to forget about our subtle energetic body. Becoming more aware of your energetic body, sometimes also called your aura, and working to strengthen it will build your capacity to do more profoundly transformational inner work.

Enhancing Your Energy – A Guided Visualization

Step One

Sit comfortably, close your eyes and take slow, deep breaths. Scan the outer edges of your body, see if you can get a sense of where your energetic body sits in relation to your physical body and set the intention to strengthen this.

Step Two

In your mind's eye, visualize droplets of light energy collecting together to form a swirl of light around you. Allow this to intensify, pulling in energy around you like a magnet.

Step Three

Visualize this swirl coming into your solar plexus area (just below your breast bone) as an intense ball of energy. Then see it move upward, bringing light to your heart, throat, third-eye and crown chakras. Exhale the light out through your crown chakra.

Step Four

When you sense that the visualization is complete, open your eyes, bring yourself gently back into the room and write down your thoughts on the page opposite.

What did your energy body look and feel like?
Example: It looked vibrant, and felt strong but a little uneven in places.

Compare how you felt before and after the visualization. What has changed?
Example: I felt ungrounded at first but more centred and clear afterward.

choice of intuitive action for the week

Commit to being mindful of your energy levels during the week ahead.
When you observe that your energetic boundaries feel weak, do this
visualization for as long as you need, and see how things shift for you.

daily intuition journal

Use the space on these pages to keep a note of your daily intuitive experiences – moments of intuitive insight, inspired action, and how these make you feel.

Feel free to relate your observations back to your underlying intention for the phase or your choice of intuitive action for the week.

Monday

Tuesday

Wednesday

Self-care Rituals

	m	t	w	th	f	s	su
_____	○	○	○	○	○	○	○
_____	○	○	○	○	○	○	○

Thursday

Friday

Saturday

Sunday

Weekly Reflection

I felt most connected to myself this week when _____

I listened most to my intuition this week when _____

The Chinese concepts of yin (receptive, traditionally feminine energy) and yang (active, traditionally male energy) are opposing forces that depend on and flow into one another, like night and day. When we look quietly inward, tune into our intuition and explore our creativity, we cultivate more yin energy; when we do more intense, active, physical work, we cultivate more yang energy.

Everyone needs a healthy balance of both to flourish in life, so let's start this week by observing where your energy is today. Place a mark on each line below to see where you fall between yin and yang states:

Today, I am:

Yin		Yang
Feeling creative and abstract	○————————○	Feeling logical and factual
Focused on the experience	○————————○	Focused on the destination
Moving at a slower pace	○————————○	Moving at a faster pace
Reflective and quiet	○————————○	Energized and assertive
Relaxed and in the flow	○————————○	Organized and productive
Receiving energy from others	○————————○	Giving energy to others
Conserving energy	○————————○	Expending energy

Based on this exercise, what is your predominant energetic state at the moment?
Circle the most appropriate.

Yin   *Yang*   *Balanced*

How does being in this energetic state make you feel?
Example: I feel tired and burnt-out from being in a predominantly yang state.

How would you like to change this in order to cultivate a little more balance?
Example: I would like to feel more relaxed and in the flow, so I need more yin energy.

choice of intuitive action for the week

Use the exercise opposite to track your changing yin and yang states
as you journey through the week ahead – in order to get a sense of
how you could bring more intuitive balance to your life.

daily intuition journal

Use the space on these pages to keep a note of your daily intuitive experiences – moments of intuitive insight, inspired action, and how these make you feel.

Feel free to relate your observations back to your underlying intention for the phase or your choice of intuitive action for the week.

Monday

Tuesday

Wednesday

Self-care Rituals

	m	t	w	th	f	s	su
_____	☐	☐	☐	☐	☐	☐	☐
_____	☐	☐	☐	☐	☐	☐	☐

Thursday	Friday

Saturday	Sunday

Weekly Reflection

I felt most connected to myself this week when _____

I listened most to my intuition this week when _____

intuition focus
Balancing your yin–yang energy

Building on the exploration of yin and yang energy in last week's Intuition Focus, let's start this week by considering simple things you could do to bring these energies into balance. Welcoming the duality of yin and yang into your life will help to strengthen your energetic body and deepen your inner work.

Identify 5 practices you could do to balance an excess of soft, receptive yin energy. *Feel free to use the suggestions opposite.*

1.

2.

3.

4.

5.

Identify 5 practices you could do to balance an excess of intense, active yang energy. *Feel free to use the suggestions opposite.*

1.

2.

3.

4.

5.

To Balance Excess Yin / Build Yang	*To Balance Excess Yang / Build Yin*
Watch the sunrise	Spend time moon-gazing
Welcome natural light into your home	Create a dark and cosy cocoon indoors
Do faster paced workouts, such as cardio, or Kundalini or Bikram yoga	Do slower paced workouts and stretches, yin yoga or yoga nidra
Make a schedule for the week	Leave downtime for yourself
Plan all meals for the week ahead	Cook intuitively
Enjoy baked, smoked or roast dishes, adding ginger and warming spices	Enjoy salads and other meals at room temperature
Create an invigorating morning ritual for yourself	Create a slow, relaxing evening ritual for yourself
Spend time in the city	Spend time in nature
Spend time with friends and family	Make time to be alone

choice of intuitive action for the week

Integrate the yin and yang practices that you have identified on the page opposite wherever relevant in the week ahead – and see how this makes you feel.

daily intuition journal

Use the space on these pages to keep a note of your daily intuitive experiences – moments of intuitive insight, inspired action, and how these make you feel.

Feel free to relate your observations back to your underlying intention for the phase or your choice of intuitive action for the week.

Monday

Tuesday

Wednesday

Self-care Rituals

	m	t	w	th	f	s	su
_____	☐	☐	☐	☐	☐	☐	☐
_____	☐	☐	☐	☐	☐	☐	☐

Thursday

Friday

Saturday

Sunday

Weekly Reflection

I felt most connected to myself this week when _____

I listened most to my intuition this week when _____

This whole final phase of your intuition growth is about flourishing – the feeling you get when you are able move through each day in flow, with a deep sense of energetic balance, purpose and connection to your higher self. So let's start this week by looking at areas of your life that you feel could do with more time, care and nourishment – in order for you to flourish as holisitically as possible.

Choose 1 area of your life that you feel needs more nourishment:

○ *Work*   ○ *Abundance*   ○ *Learning*   ○ *Relationships*

○ *Health*   ○ *Creativity*   ○ *Spirituality*   _____

                                                                   Create your own

Why do you feel that this area needs more care to bring it into balance?
Example: In health, I haven't done much to move my body recently.

Identify 3 things you could do to bring this area back into energetic balance.
Example: Make time to move my body first thing each morning.

1.

2.

3.

choice of intuitive action for the week

Integrate the three actions above as much as you can into the week ahead
and see how this starts to shift how you feel. Once this particular area of
your life feels more balanced, address other areas one at a time in the same way.

daily intuition journal

Use the space on these pages to keep a note of your daily intuitive experiences – moments of intuitive insight, inspired action, and how these make you feel.

Feel free to relate your observations back to your underlying intention for the phase or your choice of intuitive action for the week.

Monday

Tuesday

Wednesday

Self-care Rituals

	m	t	w	th	f	s	su
_____	◯	◯	◯	◯	◯	◯	◯
_____	◯	◯	◯	◯	◯	◯	◯

Thursday

Friday

Saturday

Sunday

Weekly Reflection

I felt most connected to myself this week when _____

I listened most to my intuition this week when _____

Every flower
blooms in
its own time,
according
to nature's
cycle of
growth.

Higher self versus infinite wisdom

As you tune into your intuition during this final phase of the journal, you may notice energy and guidance coming from what feels like two distinct sources: your inner, higher self and a place beyond yourself. The latter tends to feel otherwordly and is often referred to as infinite wisdom, divine wisdom or the universal source. The lists of qualities below will help to build your awareness of the difference between the two so that you can cultivate both in your life.

Qualities of Intuition
from Your Higher Self

Δ   Brings messages and guidance meant only for you

Δ   Guides you to take intuitive, inspired action and navigate difficult decisions

Δ   You can tune into this when working with the third-eye chakra

Qualities of Intuition
from Infinite Wisdom

Δ   Offers messages and guidance that are for the wider good

Δ   Allows you to read the energy of an object or situation, or receive psychic hunches

Δ   You can tune into this when working with the crown chakra

intuition focus
Integrating your growth

This week, it's time to allow some space for your feelings and insights to settle, and for further clarity to channel through. Reflect on the ways in which you have learned to strengthen and balance your energy over recent weeks in order to flourish in as many areas of your life as possible.

Then use the space below for free journalling, drawing and dreaming in any way you feel drawn to.

daily intuition journal

	Monday
Use the space on these pages to keep a note of your daily intuitive experiences – moments of intuitive insight, inspired action, and how these make you feel. Feel free to relate your observations back to your underlying intention for the phase or your choice of intuitive action for the week.	
Tuesday	*Wednesday*

Self-care Rituals

	m	t	w	th	f	s	su
_____	○	○	○	○	○	○	○
_____	○	○	○	○	○	○	○

Thursday	Friday

Saturday	Sunday

Weekly Reflection

I felt most connected to myself this week when _____

I listened most to my intuition this week when _____

intuition focus
Reviewing your Phase Four intention

Let's start this week by checking in with the intention that you reviewed in Week 42. Use this time to reflect on any changes you have noticed, no matter how small, and to explore where your intuition now tells you to channel your energy to further cultivate your intention.

How has the intention that you set served you since the review in Week 42?
Example: It has reinforced the value and depth of my regular meditation.

What has changed since the last review?
Example: I feel more energetically balanced and in flow with life.

What intuitive insights or actions have felt most in alignment with your intention so far?
Example: Releasing old beliefs has helped me to build trust in myself.

Take a moment to reflect on your experiences over the past few weeks. If you feel you have shifted your perspective, you may wish to revise your initial intention. Otherwise, rewrite your original intention to recommit to it.

My intention for Phase Four of my growth is now:

choice of intuitive action for the week

Based on your answers above, identify one new intuitive action that you could do this week to further help you and your intention to flourish.

daily intuition journal

Monday

Use the space on these pages to
keep a note of your daily intuitive
experiences – moments of intuitive
insight, inspired action, and how
these make you feel.

Feel free to relate your observations
back to your underlying intention
for the phase or your choice of
intuitive action for the week.

Tuesday

Wednesday

Self-care Rituals

	m	t	w	th	f	s	su
_____	☐	☐	☐	☐	☐	☐	☐
_____	☐	☐	☐	☐	☐	☐	☐

Thursday	Friday

Saturday	Sunday

Weekly Reflection

I felt most connected to myself this week when _____

I listened most to my intuition this week when _____

intuition focus
Channelling infinite wisdom

Starting this week with a free-journalling exercise will help you to see how your intuition can channel wisdom from the universe as well as from your higher self. The first few paragraphs or pages may feel strange. But be patient and notice how your words flow once guidance from divine wisdom starts to come through.

You will need:

Some blank paper, a pen or pencil, a timer, and trust that you will receive guidance through infinite wisdom

Before you begin

Do some of the grounding practices and cleansing rituals from Phase One to free your space of negative energy

Step One ~ Set a tone

Take a deep breathe to centre yourself and choose something that you would like guidance on, focusing on a higher purpose and how you can serve others for the greater good. Write this down at the top of your piece of paper.

Step Two ~ Start writing

Set your timer for approximately 10 minutes and then simply put pen to paper, writing any thought, feeling or observation that comes through without pausing to reflect on your words, grammar or punctuation. Finish writing either when you feel you have received adequate guidance, or when your timer goes off.

Step Three ~ Reflect on your experience

Did you notice a point when your own stream of consciousness was replaced by intuitive universal guidance? If so, what felt different?
Example: It felt like a shift from mind chatter to channeled wisdom.

Did any sense of higher, universal guidance emerge? If so, what?
Example: I was guided to calmly let go of worry and stay present in the moment.

choice of intuitive action for the week

Follow any divine guidance that has channelled through from this exercise and look out during the week ahead for moments where you feel the switch from heart-led intuition to a broader experience of infinite wisdom.

daily intuition journal

Use the space on these pages to keep a note of your daily intuitive experiences – moments of intuitive insight, inspired action, and how these make you feel.

Feel free to relate your observations back to your underlying intention for the phase or your choice of intuitive action for the week.

Monday

Tuesday

Wednesday

Self-care Rituals

	m	t	w	th	f	s	su
_____	☐	☐	☐	☐	☐	☐	☐
_____	☐	☐	☐	☐	☐	☐	☐

Thursday

Friday

Saturday

Sunday

Weekly Reflection

I felt most connected to myself this week when _____

I listened most to my intuition this week when _____

week ⟨51⟩ intuition focus
Living in energetic flow

Let's start the penultimate week of your intuition journey by exploring a range of self-care rituals that could help you increase your capacity to channel the infinite wisdom of universal energy. The more you can cultivate your ability to tap into this, the more you will be able to flourish in life – from a state of energetic flow.

List one from each of the categories of self-care practices opposite that intuitively appeal to you. Also feel free to revisit practices from previous weeks to bring together what you have learned while working through your journal.

choice of intuitive action for the week

Decide on one or more of these self-care practices to introduce into your life during the week ahead and observe how, after a while, they help to strengthen your energetic and intuitive abilities.

In Your Body

Do a gentle detox using organic foods

Explore meditative yoga postures such as Corpse Pose (*Savasana*)

Explore Kundalini yoga kriyas that move energy and cleanse your aura

Try reiki, qigong or acupuncture

In Your Mind

Make a conscious effort to release old limiting habits, beliefs and patterns

Remain open to synchronicities

Be mindful of aligning your words, intentions and thoughts to embody a sense of your higher self

In Nature

Hike to the top of a peak to see the world from a wider perspective

Diffuse essential oils such as lavender, frankincense and myrrh

Work with herbs such as peppermint, holy basil and gotu kola

Invest in crystals such as clear quartz, selenite, moonstone and white calcite

Other Rituals

Focus on being of service and value to others in every key decision you make

Take intuitive action toward things that help you to expand beyond what you thought was possible

Visualize light energy moving from the base of your spine up through your body to your third-eye chakra , then your crown chakra

daily intuition journal

Use the space on these pages to keep a note of your daily intuitive experiences – moments of intuitive insight, inspired action, and how these make you feel.

Feel free to relate your observations back to your underlying intention for the phase or your choice of intuitive action for the week.

Monday

Tuesday

Wednesday

Self-care Rituals

	m	t	w	th	f	s	su
_____	◯	◯	◯	◯	◯	◯	◯
_____	◯	◯	◯	◯	◯	◯	◯

Thursday

Friday

Saturday

Sunday

Weekly Reflection

I felt most connected to myself this week when _____

I listened most to my intuition this week when _____

intuition focus
Reflecting back on Phase Four

Now that you've reached the end of this final phase of your intuition journey, let's start the week by acknowledging and celebrating all that you have learned and nurtured over the past 12 weeks. Reflect back on how you have cultivated:

△ ways to move beyond your comfort zone

△ a stronger, more balanced energetic foundation

△ ways to recognize and channel infinite wisdom

△ enhanced creative flow and flourish

Now sit quietly, tune in to your breath and respond to these prompts:

What did you learn about how your intuition speaks to you in Phase Four?

How have you flourished from living your Phase Four intention?

3 key times your intuition guided you as you made a decision:

1.

2.

3.

3 key things you manifested by taking intuitive action:

1.

2.

3.

3 key challenges or fears you overcame by following your intuition:

1.

2.

3.

choice of intuitive action for the week

What have you done as a result of following your intuition throughout
Phase Four that you are most proud of and grateful for? And why
do you think that is? Make a choice to honour this by carrying the
energy of it into the week ahead and seeing how this makes you feel.

daily intuition journal

Use the space on these pages to keep a note of your daily intuitive experiences – moments of intuitive insight, inspired action, and how these make you feel.

Feel free to relate your observations back to your underlying intention for the phase or your choice of intuitive action for the week.

Monday

Tuesday

Wednesday

Self-care Rituals

	m	t	w	th	f	s	su
_____	☐	☐	☐	☐	☐	☐	☐
_____	☐	☐	☐	☐	☐	☐	☐

week ⟨52⟩

Thursday

Friday

Saturday

Sunday

Weekly Reflection

I felt most connected to myself this week when _____

I listened most to my intuition this week when _____

honouring the completion of your cycle of growth

Congratulations for completing this journey of self-enquiry! You should feel incredibly proud of yourself for having worked through all four phases of intuitive growth. Every intention you have set and action you have taken will have helped to strengthen your intuition and connect you to your higher self.

As you look back on the cycle of growth that you have undergone, don't worry if you didn't tick off everything you had set your sights on. There will always be more to do. The important thing is to honour all the learning so far. A seed does not hurry to become a tree, and a flower does not hurry to bloom. Everything, including your own growth and transformation, happens with exquisite timing.

As I complete this cycle of transformtional inner growth,
I want to honour and express my gratitude for:

The biggest challenge or difficult situation I have overcome:

The biggest lesson I have learned:

The most important change I see and feel within myself:

Having now completed The Intuition Journal, *you may like to continue your journey. If so, please feel free to order another journal and/or visit my website for further inspiration: TheIntuitionJournal.com.*

It is my hope that your continued exploration of intuition brings you calm, joy and clarity.

WATKINS

Sharing Wisdom Since 1893

The story of Watkins began in 1893, when scholar of esotericism John Watkins founded our bookshop, inspired by the lament of his friend and teacher Madame Blavatsky that there was nowhere in London to buy books on mysticism, occultism or metaphysics. That moment marked the birth of Watkins, soon to become the publisher of many of the leading lights of spiritual literature, including Carl Jung, Rudolf Steiner, Alice Bailey and Chögyam Trungpa.

Today, the passion at Watkins Publishing for vigorous questioning is still resolute. Our stimulating and groundbreaking list ranges from ancient traditions and complementary medicine to the latest ideas about personal development, holistic wellbeing and consciousness exploration. We remain at the cutting edge, committed to publishing books that change lives.

DISCOVER MORE AT:

www.watkinspublishing.com

Read our blog

Watch and listen to
our authors in action

Sign up to
our mailing list

We celebrate conscious, passionate, wise and happy living.
Be part of that community by visiting

 /watkinspublishing    @watkinswisdom

 /watkinsbooks    @watkinswisdom